The Imprisonment & Death of King Charles I, Related by one of his Judges

"*INVENIRE.*"

The Imprisonment & Death of King Charles I.

RELATED BY ONE OF HIS JUDGES.

BEING EXTRACTS FROM THE MEMOIRS OF

EDMUND LUDLOW, THE REGICIDE,

WITH

A Collection of Original Papers

RELATING TO THE TRIAL OF THE KING

" *You, O Books, are the golden vessels of the Temple, burning lambs to be ever held in the hand* "

RICHARD AUNGERVYLE

PRIVATELY PRINTED FOR THE AUNGERVYLE SOCIETY,
EDINBURGH

1882,

59/₆₇₄/₁₆

A 360573

Impression limited to 150, of which this is No 15:

E. M. G.

Introduction.

THE Imprisonment, Trial, and Death of Charles I. have, for nearly two centuries and a half, had an irresistible attraction for readers of all ranks and of all ages. The narratives that have been published are innumerable, but nearly all have been mere reproductions of the writings of Royalist Historians, such as Clarendon. It will no doubt be a novelty to many to see events as they appeared to one of the Regicides, and especially to one who outlived the fever passion of the Revolution, and who wrote his recollections of those stirring times many years afterwards in the calm security of his Swiss home.

Edmund Ludlow, the author of the memoirs from which the following pages are extracted, was born at Maiden Bradley, in Wilts, in 1620, and was educated at Trinity College, Oxford, He became an officer of the Parliamentary Army, and fought bravely at Edgehill and Newbury In 1645 he succeeded his father as member for Wiltshire, and warmly espoused the popular cause. His connection with the Trial of the King is clearly stated in the following pages He distinguished himself in Ireland as general of the horse under Ireton, but having opposed the nomination of Cromwell as Protector, he found it prudent to retire from public affairs On the death of Oliver Cromwell, he rejoined the army and

was mainly instrumental in recalling the Long Parliament;
but, foreseeing the Restoration, he left England and took
refuge in Switzerland   After the Revolution of 1688 he ventured back to London, but the House of Commons having
presented an address for his arrest, he retired again to Vevey
on the lake of Geneva, where he died in 1693, at the age of 72.
He was probably one of the most honest of the leaders of the
Republican party, and his Memoirs bear the impress of truth
at every page

I need only add that the edition of Ludlow's Memoirs I
have made use of is the third, printed in Edinburgh by Sands
in 1751

The almost unknown pleading that the Republicans
intended to deliver at the Bar on the Trial of the King, had
such a step been deemed necessary, and which forms one of
the original papers appended to this Reprint, is a most curious
and interesting document to all students of English History
It may be advisable to add that all the documents in the
appendix are absolutely unabridged

J. T H.

𝕿𝖍𝖊 𝕵𝖒𝖕𝖗𝖎𝖘𝖔𝖓𝖒𝖊𝖓𝖙 𝖆𝖓𝖉 𝕯𝖊𝖆𝖙𝖍

OF

𝕶𝖎𝖓𝖌 𝕮𝖍𝖆𝖗𝖑𝖊𝖘 𝕵.

RELATED BY ONE OF HIS JUDGES.

CHARLES I. left Oxford April 27th, 1646, and, accompanied by "one Hudson, and Mr Ashburnham, passing as a servant to the latter," took refuge with the Scots army. The house of Commons sent an order to their commissioners in this army, to demand the person of the King; judging it unreasonable, that the Scots army being in their pay, should assume the authority to dispose of the King otherwise than by their order; resolving further, that the King should be conducted to the castle of Warwick, and that those who came out of Oxford with him, should be brought to London. The next day they commanded their army to advance, in order to hinder the conjunction of the King's forces with the Scots. The King, soon after his arrival at the Scots quarters, gave orders for the delivery of Newark into their hands; which having received, they surrendered to the English, and marched with the King to Newcastle: whereof the house of Commons being informed, and that the Earl of Leven, General of the Scots army, had, by proclamation, forbidden his forces to have any communication with the King's party, they desisted from their resolution of advancing their army, and of conducting the King to Warwick; ordering the Scots to keep him for the parliament of England. Mr Ashburnham was permitted by the Scots to make his escape: but

Mr Hudson was brought to London , and, upon examination at the bar of the house of Commons, confessed some things about the King's journey from Oxford   Commissioners being appointed by the parliament to be sent down to the Scots army in this conjuncture, they made choice of two Lords, of whom the Earl of Pembroke was one, and four of the Commons   In which number Col. Brown the woodmonger being nominated to that employment, he turned about to me, who sat behind him in the house, assuring me that he would be ever true to us   And truly I then believed him, having met him at the beginning of the war in Smithfield buying horses for the service of the parliament , where he spoke very affectionately concerning their undertaking, and served them afterwards very successfully, especially at Abingdon, as I mentioned before.   But this wretched man soon discovered the corruption of his nature, and malignity that lay concealed in his heart   for no sooner had the King found out his ambitious temper, and cast some slight favours upon him, giving him a pair of silk stockings with his own hand, but his low and abject original and education became so prevalent in him, as to transform him into an agent and spy for the King , proving, as will be hereafter related, one of the bloodiest butchers of the parliament's friends

The Scots, having the King in their power, pressed him to write to the Earl of Ormond his Lieutenant in Ireland, and to the governors and commanders of places that remained in arms for him, to lay down their arms, and to deliver the said places to such as the parliament of England should appoint to receive them ; acquainting him, that otherwise they could not protect him   Submitting to this necessity, he sent orders to that effect , which some obeyed, and others refused to comply with, looking upon him to be under force   Amongst those who yielded obedience to the King's orders, was Montrose, who disbanded the forces he had left, and went beyond sea   The city of Oxford, having been blocked up for some time, began to capitulate, lest their farther obstinacy should prove prejudicial to them, particularly in the matter of compositions for their estates, the most considerable of the King's party being there.   Commissioners were appointed on both sides to treat , and came to an agreement on the 22d of June 1646, upon such terms as the parliament were unwilling to confirm   But whilst they were in debate concerning the articles, they understood that Prince Rupert, and others of the King's party, were marched out of the town in pursuance of them , and that the garrison would be entirely evacuated before they could signify their pleasure to the army. Wherefore, though they did not approve the conditions, yet they thought not fit to do any thing in order to break them   The principal reason given by the army of their proceeding so hastily to a conclusion of the treaty, was, lest the King should make terms with the Scots, and bring their army to the relief of Oxford   Farringdon-house, Wallingford castle, and Woodstock, were surrendered to the parliament , Worcester and Litchfield soon after, as also Pendennis and Ragland castle.

The Scots, by their commissioners, pressed the parliament to send propositions of peace to the King . wherein they were seconded by an insolent address from the Mayor and common council of the city of London , in which, after some acknowledgements of the care and courage of the parliament in the reformation of the church, and preservation of the laws, they desired of them, that such assemblies as were privately held to introduce new sects might be suppressed, lest they should breed disturbances in church and state , that they would hasten the establishment of peace in the three kingdoms , that they would consider the great services of the Scots, and dismiss those who were distinguished by the name of *Independents* from all employments civil and military, esteeming them to be firebrands that might endanger the public peace , with other particulars of the same nature. The answer of the parliament to the said address was not much to the satisfaction of the petitioners, being a positive declaration that they resolved to preserve their authority entire to themselves

The city of London had made it their request in the petition before mentioned, that some commissioners from them might accompany those from the parliament to the King , but their own party in the house, fearing perhaps to be outbid by them, or, it may be, not having quite lost all sense of honour, rejected that motion with contempt ; alledging, that they had their representatives in parliament, and were concluded by what they acted, as well as other men. Upon which Mr Martin said, That though he could not but agree

187

with what had been affirmed touching their being involved in what
their representatives did, and their not sending commissioners as
desired , yet, as to the substance of what they proposed, he could
not so much blame them as others had done , they therein shewing
themselves in the end of the war no less prudent, than they had
expressed themselves honest in the beginning For as, when the
parliament invited them to stand by them in the war against the
King, in defence of their religion, lives, liberties, and estates, they
did it heartily , and therein shewed themselves good Christians, and
true Englishmen : so now, the war being ended, and the parliament
upon making terms with the King, and thinking fit to sue to him,
now their prisoner, for peace, whom they had all incensed by their
resistance , the citizens, having considerable estates to lose, shewed
themselves prudent men, in endeavouring to procure their pardons
as well as others.   And though, said he, you will not permit them to
send as they desire, they have expressed their good will , which,
without doubt, will be well accepted   The commissioners of parliament, joining with those who were before with the King, endeavoured
to persuade him to agree to the propositions of the parliament , but
he disliking several things in them, and most of all the abolition of
Episcopacy, to which interest he continued obstinately stedfast,
refused his consent , upon private encouragement from some of the
Scots and English to expect more easy terms, or to be received without any at all   The parliament, willing to bring this matter to
a conclusion, sent the same propositions a second time to the King,
and desired the Scots to use their utmost endeavours to procure his
consent to them.   The Scots commissioners, especially the Lord
Loudon, pressed the King very earnestly to comply with them ,
telling him, that though the propositions were higher in some particulars than they could have wished, notwithstanding their endeavours
to bring them as low as they could, according to their promises , yet
if he continued to reject them, he must not expect to be received in
Scotland, whither they must return , and, upon his refusal of the
conditions offered, deliver him up to the parliament of England.
But whatsoever they or the English could say, making no impression
upon the King, the parliament's commissioners returned with a negative from him

188

The interposition of the Scots in this affair proving ineffectual, the war being at an end, and such considerable forces altogether unnecessary, the parliament appointed commissioners to confer with those of Scotland concerning such things as remained to be performed by the treasury between them, that the fraternal union might continue and the Scots depart towards their own country. In order to which, the accounts of their army were adjusted, and a great sum of money agreed to be paid to them at the present, and other sums upon certain days, to their full satisfaction. Maj.-Gen Skippon, with a considerable body of men, carried down the money *in specie* for the payment of the Scots army, which being received by them, they delivered the King into the hands of the parliament's commissioners that attended him there, and began their march for Scotland, having delivered Newcastle to the English, and drawn their men out of Berwick and Carlisle, which two places were agreed not to be garrisoned without the consent of both kingdoms.

Whilst the King was at Newcastle, the President de Bellievre came over into England in the quality of an Ambassador from the French King, with orders to endeavour a reconciliation between the King and the parliament He had a favourable audience from the two houses, and their permission to apply himself to the King But being on his way towards him, upon farther debate, they judged it not fit to subject that affair to the cognisance of any foreign prince, resolving to determine it themselves without the interposition of any, having experienced, that most of the neighbouring states, especially the monarchical, were at the bottom their enemies, and their ambassadors and residents so many spies upon them; as appeared more particularly by letters taken in the King's cabinet after the battle of Naseby, which discovered, that the Emperor's resident in London held a private correspondence with the King, and there was ground to believe, that the Ambassador of Portugal did the like, from letters therein found from that King These applications to the King, together with the permission granted by the parliament to the Turkey Company, to address themselves to him for the commissionating of one whom they had nominated to be their agent with the Grand Signior, under pretence that he would not otherwise be received, to which may be added, the frequent overtures of peace made

by the parliament to the King, though he had not a sword left
wherewith to oppose them ; and the great expectations of the people
of his return to the parliament, being informed, that the heads of the
Presbyterian party had promised the Scots, upon the delivery of the
King, that as soon as they had disbanded the army, they would bring
him to London in honour and safety these things, I say, made the
people ready to conclude, that though his designs had been wonderfully defeated, his armies beaten out of the field, and himself delivered into the hands of the parliament, against whom he had made a long
and bloody war, yet certainly he must be in the right : and that
though he was guilty of the blood of many thousands, yet was still
unaccountable, in a condition to give pardon, and not in need of
receiving any which made them flock from all parts to see him as he
was brought from Newcastle to Holmby, falling down before him,
bringing their sick to be touched by him, and courting him as only
able to restore to them their peace and settlement.

The party in the house that were betraying the cause of their
country, became encouragers of such petitioners as came to them
from the city of London, and other places, to that effect , very many
of whom had been always for the King's interest , but their estates
lying in the parliament's quarters, they secured them by their presence
in the house, and at the same time promoted his designs by their
votes. There was another sort of men, who were contented to
sacrifice all civil liberties to the ambition of the Presbyterian clergy,
and to vest them with a power as great or greater than that which
had been declared intolerable in the Bishops before To this end,
they encouraged the reduced officers of the Earl of Essex, such as
Massey, Waller, Poyntz, and others, to press the Parliament for their
arrears in a peremptory and seditious manner, that, being furnished
with money, they might be enabled to stand by these their
patrons in whatsoever design they had to carry on. And the better
to facilitate the disbanding of the army, which they so much desired,
they resolved to draw off a considerable part of them for the service
of Ireland , and to render the work more acceptable, voted Maj -
Gen Skippon to command them , joining the Earl of Warwick and
Sir William Waller in commission with Sir Thomas Fairfax, to draw
out such forces as were willing to go, to continue such as should be
190

thought necessary for the security of this nation, and to disband the rest   The army being well informed of the design, began to consult how to prevent it   And though many of the officers were prevailed with to engage, by advancements to higher commands, yet the major part absolutely refused   The commissioners of the parliament having done what they could in prosecution of their instructions, ordered those who had engaged in the Irish service, to draw off from the army, which then lay at Saffron Walden, and about Newmarket, and to be quartered in the way to Ireland   which done, they returned to London, with an account of their proceedings

The parliament being informed of what passed, were highly displeased with the carriage of the army.   But the prudence and moderation of Maj -Gen Skippon, in his report of that matter to the house, much abated the heat of their resentment   Yet some menacing expressions falling from some of them, Lt -Gen Cromwel took the occasion to whisper me in the ear, saying, " These men will never " leave till the army pull them out by the ears "   Which expression I should have resented, if the state of our affairs would have permitted.   In this conjuncture, five regiments of horse chose their agitators , who agreed upon a petition to the parliament, to desire of them to proceed to settle the affairs of the kingdom, to provide for the arrears of the army, and to declare that they would not disband any of them till these things were done ; deputing William Allen, afterwards known by the addition of Adjutant-General, Edward Sexby, afterwards Col Sexby, and one Philips, to present it, which they did accordingly at the bar of the house of Commons   After the reading of the petition, some of the members moved, that the messengers might be committed to the Tower, and the petition declared seditious   But the house, after a long debate, satisfied themselves to declare, That it did not belong to the soldiery to meddle with civil affairs, nor to prepare or present any petition to the parliament without the advice and consent of their General , to whom they ordered a letter to be sent, to desire for the future his care therein : with which acquainting the three agents, and requiring their conformity thereunto, they dismissed them   But this not satisfying, another petition was carried on throughout the army, much to the same effect , only they observed the order of the parliament,

191

in directing it to their General, desiring him to present it. The
house having notice of this combination against them from Col
Edward Harley, one of their members, who had a regiment in the
army, expressed themselves highly dissatisfied therewith; and some
of them moved, that the petitioners might be declared traitors;
alledging, that they were servants, who ought to obey, not capitulate.
Others were not wanting, who resolved the securing of Lt-Gen
Cromwel, suspecting that he had under-hand given countenance
to this design   But he being advertised of it, went that afternoon
towards the army, so that they missed of him, and were not willing
to shew their teeth, since they could do no more   The debate continued till late in the night   and the sense of the house was, that
they should be required to forbear the prosecution of the said petition
But when the house, wearied with the long sitting, was grown thin,
Mr Denzil Hollis, taking that opportunity, drew up a resolution upon
his knee, declaring the petition to be seditious, and those traitors
who should endeavour to promote it after such a day, and promising
pardon to all that were concerned therein, if they should desist by
the time limited   Some of us, fearing the consequence of these
divisions, expressed our dissatisfaction to it, and went out, which
gave them occasion to pass two or three very sharp votes against the
proceedings of the army   The agitators of the army sensible of their
condition, and knowing that they must fall under the mercy of the
parliament, unless they could secure themselves from their power by
prosecuting what they had begun, and fearing that those who had
shewed themselves so forward to close with the King, out of principle,
upon any terms, would now, for their own preservation, receive him
without any, or rather put themselves under his protection, that they
might the better subdue the army, and reduce them to obedience by
force, sent a party of horse, under the command of Cornet Joyce,
on the 4th of June 1647, with an order in writing, to take the King
out the hands of the commissioners of parliament   The Cornet,
having placed guards about Holmby-house, sent to acquaint the
King with the occasion of his coming, and was admitted into his bed-
chamber, where, upon promise that the King should be used civilly,
and have his servants and other conveniences continued to him, he
obtained his consent to go with him. But whilst Cornet Joyce was
192

giving orders concerning the King's removal, the parliament's commissioners took that occasion to discourse with the King, and persuaded him to alter his resolution. Which Joyce perceiving at his return, put the King in mind of his promise, acquainting him, that he was obliged to execute his orders. Whereupon the King told him, that since he had passed his word, he would go with him, and to that end descended the stairs to take horse. The commissioners of the parliament being with him, Col Brown and Mr Crew, who were two of them, publicly declared that the King was forced out of their hands, and so returned, with an account of what had been done, to the parliament.

The King's officers who waited on him, were continued, and the chief officers of the army began publicly to own the design, pretending thereby to keep the private soldiers (for they would no longer be called common soldiers) from running into greater extravagancies and disorders. Col Francis Russel and others, attending on the King, became soon converted by the splendor of his Majesty; and Sir Robert Pye, a Colonel in the army, supplied the place of an Equerry, riding bare before him when he rode abroad: so that the King began to promise to himself, that his condition was altered for the better, and to look upon the Independent interest as more consisting with Episcopacy than the Presbyterian; for that it could subsist under any form, which the other could not do, and therefore largely promised liberty to the Independent party, being fully persuaded how naturally his power would revive upon his restitution to the throne, and how easy it would be for him to break through all such promises and engagements, upon pretence that he was under a force. The principal officers of the army made it so much their business to get the good opinion of the King, that Whalley being sent from them with orders to use all means but constraint to cause him to return to Holmby, and the King refusing, Whalley was contented to bring him to the army. Yet, in the mean time, a charge of high treason was drawn up by the army against eleven members of the house of Commons, who were, Mr Denzil Hollis, Sir Philip Stapylton, Sir John Clotworthy, Serjeant Glynn, Mr Anthony Nichols, Mr Walter Long, Sir William Lewis, [Col Edward Harley, Commissary Copley, Col. Massey, and Sir John Maynard, for betraying the cause of the parlia-

ment, endeavouring to break and destroy the army, with other particulars   This charge they accompanied with a declaration, shewing
the reasons of what they had done , affirming, that they were obliged
by their duty to do so, as they tendered the preservation of the public
cause, and securing the good people of England from being a prey to
their enemies   The great end of this charge of treason being rather
to keep these members from using their power with the parliament
in opposition to the proceedings of the army, than from any design
to proceed capitally against them, they resolved rather to withdraw
themselves voluntarily, than to put the parliament or army to any
farther trouble, or their persons to any more hazard. By these means
the army, in which there were too many who had no other design
but the advancement of themselves, having made the parliament, the
Scots, and the city of London, their enemies, thought it convenient
to enlarge their concessions to the King , giving his chaplains leave
to come to him, and to officiate in their way, which had been denied
before   Whilst this design was on foot, I went down to their quarters
at Maidenhead, to visit the officers , where Commissary-General
Ireton, suspecting that these things might occasion jealousies of them
in me and others of their friends in parliament, desired me to be
assured of their stedfast adherence to the public interest, and that
they intended only to dispense with such things as were not material,
in order to quiet the restless spirits of the cavaliers, till they could
put themselves into a condition of serving the people effectually.   I
could not approve of their practices , but many of the chief of them
proceeding in the way they had begun, gave out, "that the intentions
" of the officers and soldiers in the army, were to establish his Majesty
" in his just rights "   The news of this being brought to the Queen
and Prince of Wales, who were in France, they dispatched Sir
Edward Ford, brother-in-law to Commissary-General Ireton, into
England, to sound the designs of the army, and to promote an
agreement between the King and them   Soon after which Mr
John Denham was sent over on the like errand   Sir John Berkeley
also, upon his return to the Queen from Holland, where he had been
ordered to condole the death of the Prince of Orange, came into
England by the same order, and to the same purpose   It was in his
instructions, to endeavour to procure a pass for Mr. John Ashburnham, to come over and assist him in his negotiation , which, with

many other particulars relating to this business, I have seen in a
manuscript written by Sir John Berkeley himself, and left in the
hands of a merchant at Geneva Being at Dieppe, in order to imbark
for England, he met with Mr William Legge, who was of the bed-
chamber to the King; and they two came over together into England
They landed at Hastings , and, being on their way towards London,
were met by Sir Allen Appesley, who had been Lieutenant-Governor
to Sir John Berkeley at Exeter, by whom he understood, that he
was sent to him from Cromwel, and some other officers of the army,
with letters and a cypher, and also particular instructions, to desire
Sir John Berkeley to remember his own discourse at a conference
with Col Lambert, and other officers, upon the surrender of Exeter :
wherein he had taken notice of the bitter invectives of those of the
army against the King's person , and, presuming that such discourses
were encouraged in order to prepare mens minds to receive an altera-
tion of the government, had said, that it was not only a most wicked,
but difficult undertaking, if not impossible, for a few men, not of the
greatest quality, to introduce a popular government, against the King,
the Presbyterians, the Nobility, Gentry, and the genius of the nation,
accustomed for so many ages to a monarchical government advising,
that, since the Presbyterians, who had begun the war upon divers
specious pretences, were discovered to have sought their own advantages, by which means they had lost almost all their power and credit ,
the Independent party, who had no particular obligations to the
crown, as many of the Presbyterians had, would make good what the
Presbytery had only pretended to, and restore the King and people
to their just and ancient rights , to which they were obliged both by
prudence and interest, there being no means under heaven more
likely to establish themselves, and to obtain as much trust and power
as subjects are capable of whereas, if they aimed at more, it would
be accompanied with a general hatred, and their own destruction.
He had orders also to let him know, that though to this discourse of
his they then gave only the hearing , yet they had since found by ex-
perience, that all, or the most part of it, was reasonable, and that
they were resolved to act accordingly, as might be perceived by what
had already passed : desiring, that he would present them humbly to
the Queen and Prince, and be a suitor to them in their names ; not

195

to condemn them absolutely, but to suspend their opinions of them,
and their intentions, till their future behaviour had made full proof
of their innocence, whereof they had already given some testimonies
to the world   and that, when he had done this office, he would re
turn to England, and be an eye-witness of their proceedings   Thus
did the army-party endeavour to fortify their interest against the
Presbyterians , who, though they were very much weakened by
the absence of the eleven members, yet, not to be altogether wanting to themselves, passed a vote, that the King
should be brought to Richmond , whither he was inclined
to go, having conceived a distrust of the army, grounded chiefly
upon the refusal of the officers to receive any honours or advantages from him ; and would not be dissuaded from this resolution,
till the army had obliged the parliament to recal their vote   After
which he insisted upon going to Windsor, much against the sense of
the army ; and could not be prevailed with to pass by the army in
his way thither   This caused them to suspect, that he hearkened
to some secret propositions from the Presbyterians, and designed
to make an absolute breach between the parliament and the army ,
which Commissary-General Ireton discerning, said these words to
him   " *Sir*, You have an intention to be arbitrator between the parlia-
" ment and us, and we mean to be so between you and the parlia-
" ment "   But the King, finding himself courted on all hands, became
so confident of his own interest, as to think himself able to turn the
scale to what side soever he pleased.   In this temper Sir John Berkeley found him, when he delivered the Queen's letters to him , which he
did, after leave obtained from Cromwel, and a confirmation received
from his own mouth of what had been communicated before to him
by Sir Allen Appesley , with this addition, that he thought no man
could enjoy his life and estate quietly, unless the King had his rights ,
which he said they had already declared to the world in general
terms, and would more particularly very speedily , wherein they would
comprise the several interests of the Royalists, Presbyterians, and
Independents, as far as they were consistent with one another.   Sir
John Berkeley endeavoured to persuade the King, that it was necessary for him, who was now in the power of the army to dissemble with
them , and proposed, that Mr. Peters might preach before him , that
   196

he would converse freely with others of the army, and gain the good
opinion of the agitators, whose interest he perceived to be very great
amongst them   But this advice made no impression upon the King.
He gave him also a relation of what had formerly passed between himself and Cromwel, whom he met near Causum, when the head quarters
were at Reading , where Cromwel told him, that he had lately seen
the tenderest sight that ever his eyes beheld, which was, the interview
between the King and his children , that he wept plentifully at the
remembrance thereof, saying, that never man was so abused as he in
his sinister opinion of the King, who, he thought, was the most
upright and conscientious of his kingdom , that they of the Independent party had infinite obligations to him, for not consenting
to the propositions sent to him at Newcastle, which would have
totally ruined them, and which his Majesty's interest seemed
to invite him to , concluding with this wish, " That God would
" be pleased to look upon him according to the sincerity of his
" heart towards the King "   With this relation the King was no
more moved than with the rest, firmly believing such expressions to
proceed from a necessity that Cromwel and the army had of him ,
without whom, he said, they could do nothing   And indeed the
King was not without reason of that opinion   for some of the principal agitators, with whom Sir John Berkeley conversed at Reading,
expressing to him their jealousy that Cromwel was not sincere for the
King, desired of him, that, if he found him false, to acquaint them
with it , promising that they would endeavour to set him right, either
with or against his will   Maj Huntington, a creature of Cromwel,
and therefore entrusted by him to command the guard about the
King, either believing him to be in earnest in his pretensions to serve
the King, or else finding the King's affairs in a rising condition,
became one of his confidents , and, by order of the King, brought
two general officers to Sir John Berkeley, recommending them to him
as persons upon whom he might rely   These two had frequent conferences with Sir John Berkeley , and assured him, that a conjunction
with the King was universally desired by the officers and agitators ,
and that Cromwel and Ireton were great dissemblers, if they were not
real in it   but that the army was so bent upon it at present, that
they durst not shew themselves otherwise , protesting, that, however

197

things might happen to change, and whatsoever others might do, they would for ever continue faithful to the King. They acquainted him also, that proposals were drawn up by Ireton, wherein Episcopacy was not required to be abolished, nor any of the King's party wholly ruined, nor the militia to be taken away from the crown, advising, that the King would with all expedition agree to them, there being no assurance of the army which they had observed already to have changed more than once. To this end they brought him to Commissary-General Ireton, with whom he continued all night debating upon the proposals before mentioned, altering two of the articles, as he saith himself in the manuscript, in the most material points · but, upon his endeavouring to alter a third, touching the exclusion of seven persons, not mentioned in the papers, from pardon, and the admission of the King's party to sit in the next parliament, Ireton told him, that there must be a distinction made between the conquerors and those that had been beaten, and that he himself should be afraid of a parliament where the King's party had the major vote. in conclusion, conjuring Sir John Berkeley, as he tendered the King's welfare, to endeavour to procure his consent to the proposals, that they might with more confidence be offered to the parliament, and all differences accommodated. Cromwel appeared, in all his conferences with Sir John Berkeley, most zealous for a speedy agreement with the King, insomuch that he sometimes complained of his son Ireton's slowness in perfecting the proposals, and his unwillingness to come up to his Majesty's sense. at other times he would wish, that Sir John Berkeley would act more frankly, and not tie himself up by narrow principles, always affirming, that he doubted the army would not persist in their good intentions towards the King.

During these transactions, the army marched from about Reading to Bedford, and the King with his usual guard to Woburn, a house belonging to the Earl of Bedford, where the proposals of the army were brought to him to peruse, before they were offered to him in public. He was much displeased with them in general, saying, That, if they had any intention to come to an accommodation, they would not impose such conditions on him. To which Sir John Berkeley, who brought them to him, answered, That he should rather suspect they

198

designed to abuse him, if they had demanded less, there being no appearance, that men, who had through so many dangers and difficulties acquired such advantages, would content themselves with less than was contained in the said proposals; and that a crown so near lost was never recovered so easily as this would be, if things were adjusted upon these terms   But the King, being of another opinion, replied, That they could not subsist without him, and that therefore he did not doubt to find them shortly willing to condescend farther, making his chief objections against the three following points. 1 The exclusion of seven persons from pardon   2. The incapacitating any of his party from being elected members of the next ensuing parliament.   3. That there was nothing mentioned concerning church government.   To the first it was answered, That when the King and the army were agreed, it would not be impossible to make them remit in that point, but if that could not be obtained, yet, when the King was restored to his power, he might easily supply seven persons living beyond the seas in such manner as to make their banishment supportable   To the second, That the next parliament would be necessitated to lay great burdens upon the people, and that it would be a happiness to the King's party to have no hand therein   To the third, That the law was security enough for the church, and that it was a great point gained, to reduce men who had fought against it, to be wholly silent in the matter   But the King, breaking away from them, said, " Well, I shall see them glad ere long to accept of more " equal terms "

About this time Mr. Ashburnham arrived, to the King's great contentment, and his instructions referring to Sir John Berkeley's, which they were to prosecute jointly, Sir John gave him what light he could into the state of affairs.   But he soon departed from the methods proposed by Sir John Berkeley, and, entirely complying with the King's humour, declared openly, that, having always used the best company, he could not converse with such senseless fellows as the agitators, that if the officers could be gained, there was no doubt but they would be able to command their own army, and that he was resolved to apply himself wholly to them.   Upon this there grew a great familiarity between him and Whalley, who commanded the guard that waited on the King, and not long after a close cor-

respondence with Cromwel and Ireton, messages daily passing from
the King to the head quarters   With these encouragements, and
others from the Presbyterian party, the Lord Lauderdale and divers
of the city of London assuring the King that they would oppose the
army to the death, he seemed so much elevated, that, when the proposals were sent to him, and his concurrence humbly desired, he, to
the great astonishment, not only of Ireton and the army, but even of
his own party, entertained them with very sharp and bitter language ,
saying, That no man should suffer for his sake , and that he repented
him of nothing so much, as that he passed the bill against the Earl
of Strafford which though it must be confessed to have been an
unworthy act in him, all things considered , yet it was no less im-
prudent, in that manner, and at that time, to mention it and that
we would have the church established according to law by the proposals   To which those of the army replied, That it was not their
work to do it , and that they thought it sufficient for them to wave
the point, and they hoped for the King too, he having already consented to the abolition of the Episcopal government in Scotland
The King said, That he hoped God had forgiven him that sin , re-
peating frequently these or the like words, " You cannot be without
" me, you will fall to ruin, if I do not sustain you " This manner
of carriage from the King being observed with the utmost amaze-
ment by many officers of the army who were present, and at least
in appearance were promoters of the agreement , Sir John Berkeley
taking notice of it, looked with much wonder upon the King, and
stepping to him, said in his ear, "Sir, You speak as if you had some
" secret strength and power which I do not know of , and since you
" have concealed it from me, I wish you had done it from these men
" also " Whereupon the King began to recollect himself, and to soften
his former discourse   But it was too late , for Col Rainsborough,
who of all the army seemed the least to desire an agreement, having
observed these passages, went out from the conference and hastened
to the army, informing them what entertainment their commissioners
and proposals had found with the King   Sir John Berkeley, being
desirous to allay this heat, demanded of Ireton, and the rest of the
officers, what they would do if the King should consent. By whom
it was answered, That they would offer them to the parliament for
their approbation   The King, having thus bid defiance to the army,
  200

thought it necessary to bend all his force against them, and especially
to strengthen their enemies in the parliament   To this end a petition
was contrived, to press them to a speedy agreement with the King,
and presented in a most tumultuous manner, by great numbers of
apprentices and rabble, backed and encouraged by many dismissed
and disaffected officers who joined with them.   Whilst the two houses
were in debate what answer to give to this insolent multitude, some
of them getting to the windows of the house of Lords, threw stones
in upon them, and threatened them with worse usage, unless they
gave them an answer to their liking, others knocked at the door
of the house of Commons, requiring to be admitted   But some of
us with our swords forced them to retire for the present, and the
house resolved to rise without giving any answer, judging it below
them to do any thing by compulsion   Whereupon the Speaker went
out of the house, but, being in the lobby, was forced back into the
chair by the violence of the insolent rabble, whereof above a thousand attended without doors, and about forty or fifty were got into
the house   So that it was thought convenient to give way to their
rage   And the Speaker demanding what question they desired to
be put, they answered, That the King should be desired to
come to London forthwith   Which question being put, they
were asked again what further they would have, they said, That he
should be invited to come with honour, freedom, and safety.
To both which I gave a loud negative, and some of the members
as loud an affirmative, rather out of a prudential compliance,
than any affection to the design on foot   By these votes, and
the coming down of divers well-affected citizens to appease them, the
tumult was somewhat allayed, and the members of parliament with
their Speaker passed through the multitude safely.   The next morning I advised with Sir Arthur Haslerig, and others, what was fittest to
be done in this conjuncture, and it was concluded, that we could
not sit in parliament, without apparent hazard of our lives, till we had
a guard for our defence; it being manifestly the design of the other
party, either to drive us away, or to destroy us.   Therefore we
resolved to betake ourselves to the army for protection, Sir Arthur
Haslerig undertaking to persuade the Speaker to go thither, to which
he consented with some difficulty   and having caused 1000 l to be
thrown into his coach, went down to the army, which lay then at

201

Windsor, Maidenhead, Colebrook, and the adjacent places. Having acquainted as many of our friends as I could with our resolution to repair to the army, I went down   And the next day, being the same to which the parliament had adjourned themselves, the army rendez-voused upon Hounslow-heath , where those members of parliament, as well Lords as Commons, who could not with safety stay at West-minster, appeared in the head of them ; at which the army ex-pressed great joy, declaring themselves resolved to live and die with them   At night, the Earl of Northumberland, the Lord Say, the Lord Wharton, and other Lords; the Speaker and members of the house of Commons aforesaid, with Sir Thomas Fairfax, and many principal officers of the army, met at Sion-house, to consult what was most advisable to do in that juncture , which whilst they were doing, an account was brought of the pro-ceedings of those at Westminster that day, by the Serjeant of the house, who came with his mace, to the no little satisfaction of the Speaker   He acquainted them, that the remaining members, being met in the house of Commons, had for some time attended the com-ing of their Speaker , but being informed, that he was gone to the army, they had made choice of one Mr Pelham, a lawyer, and mem-ber of the house, to be their Speaker   after which they had appointed a committee of Lords and Commons to join with the directors of the militia of London, in order to raise forces for the defence of the par-liament ; the success of which attempt they desired to see, before they would declare against the army   To this end, Massey, Poyntz, Brown, and Sir William Waller, encouraged by the common council, and others, who, by various artifices, had been corrupted, used all possible diligence to list men, and prepare a force to oppose the army   But their proceedings therein were much obstructed by divers honest citizens, who importunately solicited them to treat with the army , and also by the news of the general rendezvous upon Houn-slow-heath

Though the Lords had been removed from the command of the army, yet it was manifest, that their influence there still continued , partly from a desire of some great officers to oblige them, and partly from the ambition of others to be of their number , who, to shew their earnest desires to serve the King, being morally assured the par-

liament and city were likely to be shortly in the power of the army,
who might be induced to take other counsels in relation to the King
upon such success, especially considering his late carriage towards
them, they sent an express to Sir John Berkeley and Mr Ashburnham, advising, that since the King would not yield to their proposals,
that he would send a kind letter to the army, before it were known
that London would submit   Whereupon a letter was prepared immediately but the King would not sign it, till after three or four
debates, which lost one whole day's time   At last, Mr Ashburnham
and Sir John Berkeley going with it, met with messengers from the
officers to hasten it ∙ but before they could come to Sion-house, the
commissioners from London were arrived, and the letter out of season.
For coming after it was known with what difficulty it had been obtained, and that matters were like to be adjusted between the parliament and army, it lost both its grace and efficacy Notwithstanding all
which, the officers, being resolved to do what they could, proposed,
whilst the army was in the very act of giving thanks for their success,
that they should not be too much elevated therewith, but kept still
to their former engagement to the King, and once more solemnly
vote the proposals, which was done accordingly

The face of affairs in the city was at this time very various, according to the different advices they received   For upon the report of
the advance of the army, and the taking of some of their scouts, they
cried out, *Treat, Treat*   And, at another time, being informed that
men listed in great number, the word was, *Live and die, Live and die.*
But when Southwark had let in part of the army, and joined with
them, they returned to the former cry of *Treat, Treat*   To which the
Lord Mayor, Aldermen, and common council consenting, were ready
to admit the army as friends, being not able to oppose them as
enemies, and afterwards to attend those members who had retired
to the army, being in all about 100, to the parliament   Having resumed our places in the house, as many of the eleven members as
had returned to act, immediately withdrew, and Poyntz, with other
reduced officers, who had endeavoured to form a body against the
army, fled.   But we had other difficulties to encounter   For though
that vote, by which the petition of the army was declared seditious,
and those guilty of treason who should prosecute the same after such

a day, was rased out of the journal, yet, by reason that the bulk of
the opposite party was left still in the house, the militia of London
could not be changed without much difficulty, and some other votes
of great consequence could not be altered at all   However, the
parliament appointed a committee to inquire into the late force that
was put upon them, who having made their report, Sir John Maynard was impeached, and Recorder Glynn, with Mr Clement
Walker, and others, imprisoned

    A day or two after the restitution of the parliament, the army
marched through the city without offering the least violence, promising to shew themselves faithful to the public interest   But their
actions furnished occasion to suspect them, particularly, their dis-
countenancing the adjutators, who had endured the heat of the day,
the free access of all cavaliers to the King at Hampton-court, and the
public speeches made for the King by the great officers of the army
in a council of war held at Putney, some of that party taking the
same liberty in the house of Commons   where one of them publicly
said, That he thought God had hitherto blasted our counsels, because
we had dealt so severely with the cavaliers.   These things caused
many in the army, who thought themselves abused and cheated, to
complain to the council of adjutators, against the intimacy of Sir
John Berkeley and Mr Ashburnham with the chief officers of the army,
affirming, that the doors of Cromwel and Ireton were open to them,
when they were shut to those of the army   Cromwel was much
offended with these discourses, and acquainted the King's party with
them, telling Mr Ashburnham and Sir John Berkeley, that if he were
an honest man, he had said enough of the sincerity of his intentions,
and if he were not, that nothing was enough, and therefore conjured
them, as they tendered the King's service, not to come so frequently
to his quarters, but to send privately to him, the suspicion of him being
grown so great, that he was afraid to lie in them himself   This had no
effect upon Mr Ashburnham, who said, that he must shew them the
necessity of complying with the King, from their own disorders   About
three weeks after the army entered London, the Scots prevailed with
the parliament to address themselves again to the King, which was
performed in the old propositions of Newcastle, some particulars relating to the Scots only excepted   The King advising with some

about him concerning this matter, it was concluded to be unsafe for him to close with the enemies of the army whilst he was in it. Whereupon the King refused the articles, and desired a personal treaty.   The officers of the army having seen his answer before it was sent, seemed much satisfied with it, and promised to use their utmost endeavours to procure a personal treaty, Cromwel, Ireton, and many of their party in the house, pressing the King's desires with great earnestness, wherein, contrary to their expectations, they found a vigorous opposition from such as had already conceived a jealousy of their private agreement with the King, and were now confirmed in that opinion, and the suspicions of them grew to be so strong, that they were accounted betrayers of the cause, and lost almost all their friends in the parliament.   The army, that lay then about Putney, was no less dissatisfied with their conduct, of which they were daily informed by those that came to them from London so that the adjutators began to change their discourse, and to complain openly in council, both of the King, and the malignants about him, saying, that since the King had rejected their proposals, they were not engaged any further to him, and that they were now to consult their own safety and the public good, that having the power devolved upon them by the decision of the sword, to which both parties had appealed, and being convinced that monarchy was inconsistent with the prosperity of the nation, they resolved to use their endeavours to reduce the government of England to the form of a commonwealth These proceedings struck so great a terror into Cromwel and Ireton, that they thought it necessary to draw the army to a general rendez-vous, pretending to engage them to adhere to their former proposals to the King, but indeed to bring the army into subjection to them and their party, that so they might make their bargain by them, designing, if they could carry this point at the rendezvous, to dismiss the council of adjutators, to divide the army, and to send those to the most remote places who were most opposite to them, retaining near them such only as were fit for their purpose This design being discovered by the adjutators, amongst whom Colonel Rainsborough had the principal interest, they used all possible industry to prevent the general muster, which was appointed to be at Ware, supposing the separation thereupon intended to be contrary to the agreement made upon taking the King out of the hands of the parliament, and destructive to the ends which they thought it their duty to promote.

In the mean time, Cromwel having acquainted the King with his danger. protesting to him, that it was not in his power to undertake for his security in the place where he was, assuring him of his real service, and desiring the Lord to deal with him and his according to the sincerity of his heart towards the King, prepared himself to act his part at the general rendezvous. The King, being doubtful what to do in this conjuncture, was advised by some to go privately to London, and appear in the house of Lords To which it was answered, That the army being masters of the city and parliament, would undoubtedly seize the King there , and if there should be any blood shed in his defence, he would be accused of beginning a new war. Others counselled him to secure his person by quitting the kingdom Against which the King objected, That the rendezvous being appointed for the next week, he was not willing to quit the army till that was passed , because if the superior officers prevailed, they would be able to make good their engagement , if not, they must apply themselves to him for their own security The Scots commissioners also, who had been long tampering with him, took hold of this opportunity to persuade him to come to their terms, by augmenting his fears as much as they could It was also proposed, that he should conceal himself in England , but that was thought unsafe, if not impossible. Some there were who proposed his going to Jersey, which was then kept for him , but the King being told by the Earl of Lanark, that the ships provided by Sir John Berkeley for that purpose had been discovered and seized, though Sir John affirms in his papers that none were provided, that design was laid aside At last the King resolved to go to the Isle of Wight , being, as is most probable, recommended thither by Cromwel, who, as well as the King, had a good opinion of Col Hammond the Governor there. To this end, the King sent Mr William Legge to Sir John Berkeley and Mr Ashburnham, requiring them to assist him in his escape , and horses were laid at Sutton in Hampshire to that purpose On the day following, Sir John Berkeley and Mr Ashburnham waiting with horses, the King with Mr. Legge came out towards evening , and being mounted, they designed to ride through the forest, having

206

the King for their guide, but they lost the way, so that the night proving dark and stormy, and the ways very bad, they could not reach Sutton before break of day, though they hoped to have been there three hours before At Sutton they were informed, that a committee of the county was there sitting by order of the parliament; which when the King heard, he passed by that place, and continued his way towards Southampton, attended only by Mr Legge, and went to a house of the Earl of Southampton at Titchfield, having sent Sir John Berkeley and Mr. Ashburnham to Col Hammond, Governor of the Isle of Wight, with a copy of the letter left upon the table in his chamber at Hampton-court, and two other letters which he had lately received, one of them without a name, expressing great fears and apprehensions of the ill intentions of the commonwealth-party against the King, the other from Cromwel, much to the same purpose, with this addition, that, in prosecution thereof, a new guard was designed the next day to be placed about the King, consisting of men of that party He also sent by them a letter to Col Hammond, wherein, after he had expressed his distrust of the levelling part of the army, as he termed it, and the necessity lying upon him to provide for his own safety, he assured him, that he did not intend to desert the interest of the army, ordering his two messengers to acquaint him, that of all the army the King had chosen to put himself upon him, whom he knew to be a person of a good extraction, and though engaged against him in the war, yet without any animosity to his person, to which he was informed he had no aversion. that he did not think it fit to surprise him, and therefore had sent the two persons before mentioned, to advertise him of his intentions, and to desire his promise to protect the King and his servants to the best of his power, and if it should happen that he was not able to do it, then to oblige himself to leave them in as good a condition as he found them Being ready to depart with these instructions, Sir John Berkeley said to the King, that, having no knowledge of the Governor, hr could not tell whether he might not detain them in the island, and therefore advised, if they returned not the next day, that he would think no more of them, but secure his own escape Towards evening they arrived at Lymington, but could not pass by reason of a violent storm. The next morning they got over to the island, and

went directly to Carisbrook castle, the residence of the Governor;
where they were told, that he was gone towards Newport   Upon this
notice, they rode after ; and having overtaken and acquainted him
with their message, he grew pale, and fell into such a trembling, that
it was thought he would have fallen from his horse   In this con-
sternation he continued about an hour , breaking out sometimes into
passionate and distracted expressions, saying, " O Gentlemen, you
" have undone me, in bringing the King into the island, if at least
" you have brought him , and if you have not, I pray let him not
" come . for what between my duty to the King, and gratitude to him
" upon this fresh obligation of confidence, and the discharge of my
" trust to the army, I shall be confounded." Upon this they took
occasion to tell him, that the King intended a favour to him and his
posterity, in giving him this opportunity to lay a great obligation upon
him, and such as was very consistent with his relation to the army, who
had solemnly engaged themselves to the King, but if he thought otherwise, the King would be far from imposing his person upon him   But,
said the Governor, if the King should come to any mischance, what
would the army and the King say to him that had refused to receive
him? To which they answered, That he had not refused him who was
not come to him   Then, beginning to speak more calmly, he desired
to know where the King was, and wished that he had absolutely
thrown himself upon him , which made the two Gentlemen suspect
that the Governor was not for their turn   But Mr Ashburnham,
fearing what would become of the King if he should be discovered
before he had gained this point, took the Governor aside , and, after
some conference, prevailed with him to declare, That he did believe
the King relied on him as a person of honour and honesty   and
therefore he did engage himself to perform whatsoever could be
expected from a person so qualified   Mr Ashburnham replied, I
will ask no more. Then said the Governor, Let us all go to the
King, and acquaint him with it   When they came to Cowes castle,
where a boat lay to carry them over, Col Hammond took Capt
Basket the Governor of that castle with him, and gave order for a
file or two of musketeers to follow them in another boat   When they
came to the Earl of Southampton's house, Mr. Ashburnham, leaving
Sir John Berkeley below with Col. Hammond and Capt. Basket,
  208

went up to the King, and having given an account of what had passed between the Governor and them, and that he was come with them to make good what he had promised, the King striking his hand upon his breast, said, " What ! have you brought Hammond with you ? O " you have undone me, for I am by this means made fast from " stirring" Mr Ashburnham then told him, that if he mistrusted Hammond, he would undertake to secure him. To which the King replied, " I understand you well enough But if I should follow " that counsel, it would be said and believed, that he ventured his " life for me, and that I had unworthily taken it from him ," telling him further, "That it was now too late to think upon anything, " but going through the way he had forced upon him , wondering " how he could make so great an oversight " At which expression Mr Ashburnham, having no more to say, wept bitterly In the mean time, Col Hammond and Capt Basket beginning to be impatient of their long attendance below in the court, Sir John Berkeley sent a Gentleman of the Earl of Southampton's to desire that the King and Mr Ashburnham would remember that they were below. About half an hour after, the King sent for them up, and before Col Hammond and Capt Basket had kissed the King's hands, he took Sir John Berkeley aside, and said to him, " Sir John, " I hope you are not so passionate as Jack Ashburnham. Do you " think you have followed my directions ? ' He answered, " No " indeed But it is not my fault, as Mr Ashburnham can tell you, " if he please ' The King, perceiving that it was now too late to take other measures, received Col. Hammond cheerfully, who, having repeated to him what he had promised before, conducted them over to Cowes The next morning the King went with the Governor to Carisbrook, and on the way thither was met by divers Gentlemen of the island by whom he understood, that the whole island was unanimously for him, except the Governors of the castles, and Col Hammond's Captains, that Hammond might be easily gained, if not more easily forced, the castle being day and night full of the King's party, and that the King might chuse his own time of quitting the island, having liberty to ride abroad daily So that not only the King and those that were with him, but also his own party, approved of the choice he had made. The King and Mr Ash-

209

burnham applied themselves to the Governor with so good success,
that he and those with him seemed to desire nothing more of the
King than to send a civil message to both houses, signifying his pro
pensity to peace, which was done accordingly

No sooner was the King's escape taken notice of by the guards,
but Col Whalley hastened to the parliament with the letter which
the King had left upon his table, shewing the reasons of his with-
drawing, and his resolution not to desert the interest of the army
And though it was visible that the King made his escape by the
advice of Cromwel, and therefore in all appearance with the consent
of Whalley, yet he pretended for his excuse to the parliament, that Mr.
Ashburnham had broken his engagement to him at his first coming
to Woburn, whereby he had undertaken, that the King should not
leave the army without his knowledge and consent.   Upon this
advice, the parliament declared it treason for any person to conceal
the King   But the manner of his escape being soon after discovered,
and that he had put himself into the hands of the Governor of the
Isle of Wight, they sent a messenger to the island for Mr Ashburnham, Sir John Berkeley, and Mr Legge, but the Governor refused
to deliver them

The time for the general rendezvous of the army being now come,
the commonwealth-party amongst them declared to stand to their
engagement, not to be dispersed till the things they had demanded
were effected, and the government of the nation established.   To
make good which resolution, several regiments appeared in the field
with distinguishing marks in their hats.   But Lt-Gen Cromwel, not
contenting himself with his part in an equal government, puffed up
by his successes to an expectation of greater things, and having driven
a bargain with the grandees in the house, either to comply with the
King, or to settle things in a factious way without him, procured a
party to stand by him in the seizing some of those who appeared
at the rendezvous in opposition to his designs.   To this end, being
accompanied with divers officers whom he had preferred, and by that
means made his creatures, he rode up to one of the regiments which
had the distinguishing marks, requiring them to take them out
which they not doing, he caused several of them to be seized, and
210

then their hearts failing, they yielded obedience to his commands
He ordered one of them to be shot dead upon the place, delivering
the rest of those whom he had seized, being eleven in number,
into the hands of the Marshal; and having dispersed the army to
their quarters, went to give an account of his proceedings to the
parliament   And though when an agreement with the King was
carried on by other hands, he could countenance the army in
opposition to the parliament, yet, now the bargain for the people's
liberty being driven on by himself, he opposed those who laboured to
obstruct it, pretending his so doing to be only in order to keep the
army in subjection to the parliament, who, being very desirous to
have this spirit suppressed in the army by any means, not only
approved what he had done, but gave him the thanks of the house
for the same   Whereunto, though single, I gave as loud a *No* as I
could, being fully convinced that he had acted in this manner for no
other end but to advance his own passion and power into the room
of right and reason; and took the first opportunity to tell him, that
the army having taken the power into their hands, as in effect they
had done, every drop of blood shed in that extraordinary way would
be required of them, unless the rectitude of their intentions and
actions did justify them, of which they had need to be very careful

The chief officers of the army having subdued those of their body
who upon just suspicion had opposed the treaty with the King,
thought themselves obliged by their former engagement to press for
a personal treaty with him, which they procured to be offered, in case
he would grant four preliminary bills.   The first of which contained
the revocation of all proclamations against the parliament   the second,
to make void all such titles of honour as had been granted by the King
since he had left the parliament, and that for the future none should
be conferred on any person without the consent of parliament, the
third was a bill to except some persons from pardon and the fourth, for
investing the militia in the two houses. All which those who thought it
reasonable and necessary to proceed judicially with him, were afraid
he would grant; it being visible, that had he been restored to the
throne upon any terms, he might easily have gratified his friends, and
revenged himself upon all his enemies. Col. Hammond and Mr.

Ashburnham had frequent conferences with the King, who had made
such promises to the Colonel, that he declared himself extremely
desirous that the army might resume their power, and clear themselves
of the coadjutors, whose authority he said he had never approved.
To this end, he sent one Mr Traughton, his chaplain, to the army,
to persuade them to make use of their success against the adjutators,
and two or three days after earnestly moved the King to send some
of those about him to the army, with letters of compliment to the
General, and others of greater confidence to Cromwel and Ireton,
promising to write to them himself, which he did, conjuring them by
their engagements, their honour and conscience, to come to a speedy
agreement with the King, and not to expose themselves to the fan-
tastic giddiness of the adjutators Sir John Berkeley was made
choice of for this employment, who, taking Mr Henry Berkeley his
cousin-german with him, departed from the island with a pass from
the Governor of Cowes, and, being on his way, met Mr Traughton
on his return, between Bagshot and Windsor, who acquainted him,
that he had no good news to carry back to the King, the army having
taken new resolutions touching his person Being gone a little farther, he was met by Cornet Joyce, who told him, that he was astonished at his design of going to the army, acquainting him, that it had
been debated amongst the adjutators, Whether, in justification of
themselves, the King should be brought to a trial? of which opinion
he declared himself to be, not out of any ill-will, as he said, to the
King's person, but that the guilt of the war might be charged upon
those that had caused it About an hour after his arrival at Windsor, Sir John Berkeley went to the General's quarters, where he found
the officers of the army assembled and, being admitted, delivered
his letters to the General, who, having received them, ordered him
to withdraw After he had attended about half an hour, he was
called in again, and told by the General, with some severity on his
face, that they were the parliament's army, and therefore could say
nothing to the King's motion about peace, but must refer those
matters, and the King's letters, to their consideration Then Sir
John looked upon Cromwel, Ireton, and the rest of his acquaintance,
who saluted him very coldly, shewing him Hammond's letter to them,
and smiling with disdain upon it Being thus disapppointed, he
212

went to his lodging, and staid there from four till six of the clock, without any company, to his great dissatisfaction   At last, he sent out his servant, with orders to find out, if possible, some of his acquaintance, who met with one that was a general officer, by whom he was ordered to tell his master, that he would meet him at midnight, in a close behind the Garter-inn   At the time and place appointed they met, where the officer acquainted him in general, that he had no good news to communicate to him, and then descending to particulars, said, " You know that I and my friends " engaged ourselves to you   that we were zealous for an agreement ; "and if the rest were not so, we were abused : that, since the tumults "in the army, we did mistrust Cromwel and Ireton, whereof I " informed you   I come now to tell you, that we mistrust neither, "and that we are resolved, nothwithstanding our engagement, to " destroy the King and his posterity   To which end Ireton has " made two propositions this afternoon   one, That you should be " sent prisoner to London, the other, That none should speak with " you upon pain of death, and I do now hazard my life by doing it " The way designed to ruin the King is, to send 800 of the most " disaffected in the army to secure his person, and then to bring him " to a trial, and I dare think no farther   This will be done in ten " days, and therefore, if the King can escape, let him do it, as he " loves his life "   Sir John then asking the reason of this change, seeing the King had done all things in compliance with the army, and that the officers were become superior since the last rendezvous ; he replied, That he could not certainly tell ; but conceived the ground of it to be, that though one of the mutineers, as he called him, was shot to death, eleven more made prisoners, and the rest in appearance overawed, yet they were so far from being so indeed, that two thirds of the army had been since with Cromwel and Ireton, to tell them, That though they were certain to perish in the enterprize, they would leave nothing unattempted to bring the whole army to their sense, and that, if all failed, they would make a division in the army, and join with any who would assist them in the destruction of those that should oppose them   that Cromwel and Ireton argued thus · If the army divide, the greatest part will join with the Presbyters, and will, in all likelihood, prevail, to our ruin, by forcing us to make our applications to the King, wherein we shall rather beg than offer any

assistance, which if the King shall give, and afterwards have the good
fortune to prevail, if he shall then pardon us, it will be all we can pre
tend, and more than we can certainly promise to ourselves, thereupon
concluding, that, if they could not bring the army to their sense, that
it was best to comply with them, schism being utterly destructive to
both   In pursuance of this resolution, Cromwel bent all his thoughts
to make his peace with the party that was most opposite to the King;
acknowledging, as he knew well how to do on such occasions, that
the glory of this world had so dazzled his eyes, that he could not discern clearly the great works that the Lord was doing   He sent also
comfortable messages to the prisoners that he had seized at the general
rendezvous, with assurances that nothing should be done to their
prejudice   And by these and the like arts he perfected his reconciliation. For my own part, I am inclined to believe, that his
son Ireton never intended to close with the King, but only to lay his
party asleep, whilst they were contesting with the Presbyterian interest in parliament   And now having secured themselves of the city,
and persuaded the King to deny the propositions of the parliament,
subdued the army, and freed themselves from the importunity of the
King and his party, they became willing to quit their hands of him,
since their transactions with him had procured them so much opposition, and to leave the breach with him upon the parliament, where
they found the Presbyterian party averse to an agreement with him
upon any proposals of the army, and the commonwealth party resolved
not to treat with him upon any at all

Sir John Berkeley being returned to his lodging, dispatched his
cousin Henry Berkeley to the Isle of Wight with two letters, one to
the Governor. containing a general relation, and doubtful judgment
of things in the army, another in cypher, with a particular account
of the foresaid conference, and a most passionate supplication to the
King to meditate nothing but his immediate escape   The next
morning he sent Col. Cooke to Cromwel, to let him know, that he
had letters and instructions to him from the King, who returned, in
answer, by the messenger, that he durst not see him, it being very
dangerous to them both; bidding him be assured, that he would
serve the King as long as he could do it without his own ruin, but
desired that it might not be expected, that he should perish for

214

his sake. Having received this answer, Sir John took horse for London, resolving not to acquaint any with the inclinations of the army, or with the King's intended escape, which he presumed would be in a few days, the Queen having sent a ship to that purpose, and pressed it earnestly in her letters. The next day after his arrival at London, he received a message from the Scots Lords Lanark and Lauderdale, desiring a meeting with him, presuming he had a commission from the King to treat but he acquainting them, that the King had said at his parting from him, that he would make good whatsoever he should undertake to any person in his name, the Lord Lanark replied, he would ask no other commission from him. At their second meeting they came near to an agreement, and resolved to conclude on the Monday following But the next day Sir John Berkeley receiving a letter from Mr Ashburnham, requiring him in the King's name to lay aside all other business, and to return immediately to the King, was constrained to go out of town that night, and to leave the treaty unfinished, to the great dissatisfaction of both parties. At his return to the island he found the King determined not to attempt his escape till he had concluded with the Scots, who, he said, being very desirous to have him out of the hands of the army, would on that account come to an accommodation upon reasonable conditions · whereas, if he should leave the army before any agreement with the Scots, they would never treat with him but upon their own terms To this end, the King ordered Sir John Berkeley, Mr Ashburnham, Dr Hammond, and Mr Legge, to review the papers relating to the treaty with the Scots, which had been managed in London chiefly by Dr Gough, a Popish priest, who, in the Queen's name, had conjured the King to make his speedy escape, and in his own beseeched him not to insist too nicely upon terms in the present exigency of his affairs But Mr Ashburnham hesitated much upon many expressions in the articles relating to the covenant, and Church of England, of which he was a zealous professor, making many replies and alterations, and at last insisted, that the King would send for the Scots commissioners to come to him Accordingly Sir William Fleming was sent to that purpose. And the next day after an express came from the said Commissioners to the King, desiring the two papers might be drawn, the one to contain the least he would be contented with, and the other the utmost that he would grant to the

Scots ; which last they desired he would sign, promising to do the
like to the first, and to deliver it to Dr Gough upon the reception of
his paper so signed   But this matter was delayed so long, that they
concluded the Scots commissioners would be on their way before
another express could be gone out of the island   At the same time
that the Scots were coming to the King, commissioners were also
sent to him by the parliament, with offers of a personal treaty, on
condition that the King, in testimony of his future sincerity, would
grant the four preliminary bills formerly mentioned   Whilst these
two sorts of commissioners were one day attending the King, as he
walked about the castle, they observed him throw a bone before two
spaniels that followed him, and to take great delight in seeing them
contesting for it , which some of them thought to be intended by him
to represent that bone of contention he had cast between the two
parties   It was proposed by some of his party, that the King should
give a dilatory answer to the Scots, that he might have the better
opportunity to escape , and at the same time it was moved, that he
should offer the four following bills to the parliament, upon presumption that they could not well refuse them, nor durst grant them   The
first was for the payment of the army, and for their disbanding as soon
as paid   the second, to put a period to the present parliament   the
third, to restore the King and Queen to the possession of their
revenues · the fourth, to settle a church-government without any
coercive power , and, till such a government were agreed on, the
present to continue without any coercive authority   This they
advised upon apprehensions, if the King should give a positive denial,
that the commissioners might have orders to injoin the Governor to
keep a stricter guard over his person, and thereby his designed
escape be prevented   To this advice the King replied, That he had
found out a remedy against their fears , which was, to deliver
his answer to the commissioners sealed up   The next day after the
English commissioners had delivered their message, and desired the
King's answer within three or four days, the commissioners of Scotland, Loudon, Lanark, Lauderdale, and others, delivered a protestation to the King, subscribed by them, against the parliament's message,
affirming it to be contrary to the covenant, being sent without their
participation or consent; and from this time began seriously to treat
with the King, concluding at last upon such terms as they could ob-
216

tain, rather than such as they desired from him. When the time to receive the King's answer was come, he sent for the English commissioners : and, before he delivered his answer, demanded of the Earl of Denbigh, who was the principal commissioner, whether they had power to alter any of the substantial or circumstantial parts of the message , and they replying, That they had not , he delivered his answer sealed up into the hands of the Earl of Denbigh. Having received the King's answer, the commissioners withdrew for a little time ; and, being returned, the Earl of Denbigh seemed to be offended, that the King had delivered his message sealed , alledging, that they were required by their instructions to bring his answer, which, whether his letter were or no, they could not know, unless they might see it , saying, that he had been his ambassador, and in that employment would never have delivered any letter without a preceding sight of it   The King told him, That he had employed twenty ambassadors, and that none of them had ever dared to open his letters . but having demanded, whether what the Earl of Denbigh had said were the sense of them all, and finding it so to be, " Well then, (said the King), I will shew it you, on condition you will " promise not to acquaint any one with the substance of it, before you " have delivered it to the parliament , " which they consenting to, he desired the company might withdraw. The commissioners proposed, that the Governor, Col. Hammond, might be permitted to stay, which the King being unwilling to allow, yet not thinking it convenient to refuse, gave way to , and by this means the Governor, as well as the commissioners, came to understand, that the King had waved the interests both of the parliament and army, to close with the Scots ; the substance of his letter being an absolute refusal of his consent to the four bills presented to him. The impression which the discovery of these things made upon the Governor was so great, that, before he departed from Carisbrook, to accompany the parliament's commissioners to Newport, he gave orders for a strict guard to be kept in his absence , and, at his return, commanded the gates to be locked up, and the guards to be doubled, sitting up himself with them all night ; whereby the King's intended escape was obstructed. The next morning he ordered the King's servants to remove, not excepting Dr. Hammond his own kinsman , who, taking leave of the King, acquainted him, that they had left the Captain of the frigat, and two

trusty Gentlemen of the island, to assist him in his escape, assuring
him they would have all things in readiness on the other side of the
water to receive him.   At their departure the King commanded them
to draw up a declaration, and send it to him the next morning to
sign , which they did, and it was afterwards published in the King's
name   When they came to Newport, one Capt Burleigh caused a
drum to beat, to draw people together in order to rescue the King .
but there were few, besides women and children, that followed him,
having but one musket amongst them all , so that the King's servants
thought not fit to join with or encourage them , but went over to the
other side, where they continued about three weeks expecting the
King's arrival , leaving Capt Burleigh, who, with divers of his fol-
lowers, was committed to jail.   Upon the return of the King's negative to the four previous bills before mentioned, the parliament voted,
" That no further addresses should be made to the King by themselves,
" or any other person, without the leave of both houses , and that if
" any presumed so to do, they should incur the guilt of high treason."
They also published a declaration, prepared by Col. Nathanael Fienes,
shewing the reasons of their said resolutions , wherein, amongst other
miscarriages of the King's reign, was represented his breaking of
parliaments, the betraying of Rochelle, his refusal to suffer any
inquiry to be made into the death of his father, his levying war
against the people of England, and his rejecting all reasonable offers
of accommodation, after six several applications to him on their part
Col. Rainsborough was appointed Admiral of the fleet , and Mr.
Holland, myself, and another member of the house of Commons, sent
down to the head quarters at Windsor, with orders to discharge from
custody Capt Reynolds, and some others called in derision *levellers*,
who had been imprisoned by the army for attempting to bring about
that which they themselves were now doing , and to exhort the officers to contribute the best of their endeavours towards a speedy
settlement

The Scots, in pursuance of their treaty with the King, made what
preparations they could to raise an army ; wherein the Presbyterians
and cavaliers joined, though with different designs.   The same spirit
began to appear also in England , many of our ships revolting to the
King, at the instigation of one Capt. Batten, who had been Vice-

Admiral to the parliament, and others, encouraged by the city and the Presbyterian party The seamen on board the ship commanded by Col. Rainsborough, refused to receive him , having before-hand secured one of my brothers, with others, whom they suspected to be faithful to their commander The Earl of Warwick, as most acceptable to them, was appointed to go down to reduce them to obedience , by which means part of the fleet was preserved to the parliament, who immediately issued out orders for the fitting out of more ships to reinforce them With the revolted ships Prince Charles blocked up the mouth of the river , and, about the same time, his brother the Duke of York, who, upon the surrender of Oxford, had been brought by order of the parliament to St James's, and provision made for him there, escaped from thence to serve the King's designs. The castles of Deal and Sandwich declared also for the King , and Col. Rich was sent with a party of the army to reduce them In the mean time, Lt-Gen. Cromwel, not forgetting himself, procured a meeting of divers leading men amongst the Presbyterians and Independents, both members of parliament and ministers, at a dinner in Westminster, under pretence of endeavouring a reconciliation between the two parties But he found it a work too difficult for him to compose the differences between these two ecclesiastical interests , one of which would endure no superior, the other no equal . so that this meeting produced no effect Another conference he contrived to be held in King-street, between those called grandees of the house and army, and the commonwealth's men , in which the grandees, of whom Lt-Gen Cromwel was the head, kept themselves in the clouds, and would not declare their judgments either for a monarchical, aristocratical, or democratical government , maintaining, that any of them might be good in themselves, or for us, according as Providence should direct us The commonwealth's men declared, that monarchy was neither good in itself, nor for us That it was not desirable in itself, they urged from the 8th chapter and 8th verse of the 1st book of *Samuel;* where the rejecting of the judges, and the choice of a King, was charged upon the Israelites by God himself as a rejection of him ; and from another passage in the same book, where Samuel declares it to be a great wickedness , with divers more texts of scripture to the same effect. And that it was no way conducing to the interest of this nation, was endeavoured to be proved by the infinite

219

mischiefs and oppressions we had suffered under it, and by it : that indeed our ancestors had consented to be governed by a single person, but with this proviso, That he should govern according to the direction of the law, which he always bound himself by oath to perform · that the King had broken this oath, and thereby dissolved our allegiance, protection and obedience being reciprocal. that having appealed to the sword for the decision of the things in dispute, and thereby caused the effusion of a deluge of the people's blood, it seemed to be a duty incumbent upon the representatives of the people, to call him to an account for the same; more especially since the controversy was determined by the same means which he had chosen, and then to proceed to the establishment of an equal commonwealth, founded upon the consent of the people, and providing for the rights and liberties of all men, that we might have the hearts and hands of the nation to support it, as being most just, and in all respects most conducing to the happiness and prosperity thereof Notwithstanding what was said, Lt-Gen. Cromwel, not for want of conviction, but in hopes to make a better bargain with another party, professed himself unresolved, and, having learned what he could of the principles and inclinations of those present at the conference, took up a cushion, and flung it at my head, and then ran down the stairs, but I overtook him with another, which made him hasten down faster than he desired   The next day, passing by me in the house, he told me he was convinced of the desirableness of what was proposed, but not of the feasibleness of it, thereby, as I suppose, designing to encourage me to hope, that he was inclined to join with us, though unwilling to publish his opinion, lest the grandees should be informed of it, to whom I presume he professed himself to be of another judgment

Much time being spent since the parliament had voted no more addresses to be made to the King, nor any messages received from him, and yet nothing done towards bringing the King to a trial, or the settling of affairs without him ; many of the people, who had waited patiently hitherto, finding themselves as far from a settlement as ever, concluded, that they should never have it, nor any ease from their burdens and taxes, without an accommodation with the King, and therefore entered into a combination through England, Scotland,

and Ireland, to restore him to his authority. To this end petitions were promoted throughout all countries, the King, by his agents, fomenting and encouraging this spirit by all means possible, as appeared by his intercepted letters. So that Lt-Gen Cromwel, who had made it his usual practice to gratify enemies even with the oppression of those who were by principle his friends, began again to court the commonwealth-party, inviting some of them to confer with him at his chamber. with which acquainting me the next time he came to the house of Commons, I took the freedom to tell him, that he knew how to cajole, and give them good words, when he had occasion to make use of them, whereat breaking out into a rage, he said, they were a proud sort of people, and only considerable in their own conceits. I told him, it was no new thing to hear truth calumniated, and that, though the commonwealth-men were fallen under his displeasure, I would take the liberty to say, that they had always been, and ever would be, considerable, where there was not a total defection from honesty, generosity, and all true virtue, which I hoped was not yet our case

The Earl of Warwick, with the fleet equipped for him by the parliament, fell down the river towards the ships commanded by Prince Charles, who presuming either that he would not fight him, or perhaps come over to him, lay some time in expectation, but finding, by the manner of his approach, that he was deceived in that particular, he thought it convenient to make all the sail he could for the coast of Holland. Our fleet followed him as far as the Texel, but, according to the defensive principle of the Nobility, our Admiral, thinking he had sufficiently discharged his duty, by clearing the Downs, and driving the other fleet from our coast, declined to fight, though he had an opportunity to engage. Deal and Sandwich castles were reduced by Col Rich, and many of our revolted ships, not finding things according to their expectation, being constrained to serve under Prince Rupert, instead of the Lord Willoughby, who they desired might command them, returned to the obedience of the parliament.

The Scots making all possible preparations to raise an army for the restitution of the King, Sir Thomas Glenham and Sir Marmaduke

221

Langdale went to Scotland to join with them in that enterprize, and
to draw what English they could to promote the design The first
of these seized upon Carlisle by order of the Scots, though contrary
to their articles Whereupon the parliament, thinking it necessary to
provide for the security of Berwick, placed a good garrison therein;
and, resolving to reinforce the militia of each county, sent down some
of their members to give life to the preparations. Amongst others I
was appointed to go down to the county for which I served; where
we agreed to raise two regiments of foot, and one of horse. In the
mean time, the enemy was not idle; and, taking advantage of the
discontents of Capt Poyer, Governor of Pembroke, they prevailed
with him to revolt, and declare for the King Other disaffected parts of
the nation, not yet ready for open opposition, acted with more caution,
preparing and encouraging petitions to the parliament for a personal
treaty with the King; of which the principal were Surrey, Essex, and
Kent. In Essex they met at Chelmsford in a tumultuous manner,
and seized Sir William Masham, and other members of parliament;
who, being ready to use all gentle methods to prevent farther incon
veniences, sent down Mr Charles Rich, second son to the Earl of
Warwick, and Sir Harbottle Grimston, two of their members, to
endeavour to quiet that tumultuous spirit, with instructions and power
to promise indemnity to all that should desist from the prosecution of
what they desired in this violent way Which commission they managed so well, that, upon the promise to present the requests of the
petitioners, which were drawn up in writing, to the parliament, and to
return them an answer, the people of the country dispersed themselves
to their own houses. But the sedition of the Surrey men was not
terminated so easily, of whom many hundreds came to the doors of
the parliament and not being satisfied with the answer the parliament thought fit to give to their petition, after they had been heated
with drink, and animated by the cavalier-party, they resolved to force
from them another answer, and, with intolerable insolence, pressed
upon their guard, beating the sentinels to the main guard, which was
drawn up at the upper end of Westminster-hall, where they wounded
the officer who commanded them, and, being intreated to desist,
became more violent. so that the soldiers were necessitated, in their
own defence, and discharge of their duty, to fire upon them, whereby

two or three of the country-men were killed. Neither did this quiet them, till some horse and foot arrived to strengthen the guard, and dispersed them. Lt-Col Cobbet, who commanded the guard, being called into the house to give an account of what had passed, went to the bar bleeding from the wounds which he had received, and related the passages before mentioned But some friends of the petitioners within doors informing the house, that the matter of fact was otherwise than had been represented by the Lieutenant-Colonel, the parliament appointed a committee to examine the truth of it.

Those of the secluded members who were in England being returned to the house, divers hard words passed between them and others of the parliament. And one day Commissary-General Ireton speaking something concerning them, Mr. Hollis, thinking it to be injurious to them, passing by him in the house, whispered him in the ear, telling him it was false, and he would justify it to be so if he would follow him ; and thereupon immediately went out of the house, with the other following him Some members who had observed their passionate carriage to each other, and seen them hastily leaving the house, acquainted the parliament with their apprehensions : whereupon they sent their Serjeant at Arms to command their attendance , which he letting them understand as they were taking boat to go to the other side of the water, they returned ; and the house taking notice of what they were informed concerning them, injoined them to forbear all words or actions of enmity towards each other, and to carry themselves for the future as fellow-members of the same body , which they promised to do

Lt-Gen Cromwel, perceiving the clouds to gather on every side, complained to me, as we were walking in the Palace-yard, of the unhappiness of his condition, having made the greatest part of the nation his enemies, by adhering to a just cause But that which he pretended to be his greatest trouble, was, that many who were engaged in the same cause with him, had entertained a jealousy and suspicion of him ; which he assured me was a great discouragement to him ; asking my advice what method was best for him to take. I could not but acknowledge that he had many enemies for the sake of the cause in which he stood engaged ; and also, that many who were

223

friends to that cause, had conceived suspicions of him. But I observed to him, that he could never oblige the former, without betraying that cause wherein he was engaged, which if he should do upon the account of an empty title, riches, or any other advantages, how those contracts would be kept with him, was uncertain ; but most certain it was, that his name would be abominated by all good men, and his memory be abhorred by posterity. On the other side, if he persisted in the prosecution of our just intentions, it was the most probable way to subdue his enemies, to rectify the mistakes of those that had conceived a jealousy of him, and to convince his friends of his integrity that if he should fall in the attempt, yet his loss would be lamented by all good men, and his name be transmitted to future ages with honour. He seemed to take well what I said; and it might have been no disservice to him, if he had acted accordingly. But his design was rather to persuade me, for the present, of the rectitude of his intentions, than to receive counsel from me concerning his conduct

About this time we obtained some advantages in Ireland, where Col Michael Jones, who had been ordered by the parliament to command at Dublin when the Earl of Ormond delivered it up, with the forces he had, fought the rebels, though double his number, at Dungon-hill, killed some thousands of them, and totally routed the rest Of which when the parliament had received information, they ordered 500 l by year of the forfeited lands in Ireland to be settled upon Col Jones, as a reward for his good service. In England the defection began to increase, Capt Henry Lilburn, who commanded for the parliament in Tinmouth castle, which lies at the mouth of the harbour, and is a key to Newcastle, declared for the King But notice thereof being brought to Sir Arthur Haslerig at Newcastle, of which town he was Governor, he, with great expedition, drew down a party before the place, and, attacking it unexpectedly, took it by assault, before the men had been thoroughly confirmed in their revolt by the Governor, whom he put to the sword, and placed another garrison therein.

Many of those who had been for the parliament in South-Wales now joining with the King's party, they grew to be a considerable body, whereby Maj.-Gen. Laughern, who, upon some suspicion, had been under confinement, was encouraged to get away, and join himself to them; Maj.-Gen John Stradling, Sir Henry Stradling, Col. Thomas Stradling, and several other Gentlemen of those parts, falling in with them   Col Horton, with about 2500 horse, foot, and dragoons, was sent into Wales to engage them, Lt-Gen Cromwel following with as many more forces as could be spared from the army; who, being within three or four days march of Col. Horton, received advice, that the enemy, to the number of about 7000, had engaged the Colonel at St. Faggons in Glamorganshire, that, upon the first attack, our forces gave ground, but well considering the danger they were in, the country being full of enemies, and encouraged by their affection to the cause wherein they were engaged, they charged the enemy's van, consisting of the best of their men, with so great bravery and resolution, that they forced them to give way, which those that were in the rear, who were for the most part new-raised men, perceiving, began to shift for themselves   Upon this ours followed their charge with so much vigour and success, that the whole body of the enemy was soon routed and dispersed   Many of them were killed in the pursuit, and many taken prisoners, amongst the latter was Maj Gen Stradling, and divers other officers   The news of this success was very welcome to all those that wished well to the public, and proved a great discouragement to the contrary party

The petitioners of Surrey drew into a body, and, in conjunction with the Kentish men of the King's party, appointed their rendezvous upon Blackheath   But Sir Thomas Fairfax, with that part of the army which he had with him, disappointed that design, by possessing himself of the ground before them   However, the enemy had brought together a considerable body of men, many of whom were induced to come in, upon assurances given that they should be commanded by Mr Hales, a Gentleman of great estate in Kent; though afterwards the Lord Goring appeared at the head of them, as had been designed from the beginning   Upon the advance of Sir Thomas Fairfax's army, the enemy, who exceeded him in number by one half at least, divided their body, sending one part to possess themselves of Maidstone, and the adjacent places, and another party to block up Dover and other forts upon the coast, whilst Goring remained with

the rest about Rochester Sir Thomas Fairfax resolving first to
attack those about Maidstone, fell upon them, and beat them into the
town, which they had fortified before whereupon though the numbers
within the town being at least equal to those without, made it a work
of great hazard and difficulty ; yet, considering that those with the
Lord Goring exceeded either, and might march to the enemy's relief,
ours resolved to storm the place, which they did the night following ,
the General, by his own example, encouraging the men to fall on ,
who for a good while were not able to make any considerable progress,
till Col Hewson, with his regiment, opened a passage into one of the
streets , where the dispute growing hot, he was knocked down with a
musket ; but recovering himself, he pressed the enemy so hard, that
they were forced to retreat to their main guard ; and, falling in with
them at the same time, so disordered them, that they all began to
shift for themselves ; wherein they were favoured by the advantage
of the night , yet many of them were made prisoners, and many
killed. Many horses, and all their artillery, fell into the hands of
ours The General, as soon as he had refreshed his men, advanced
towards that body commanded by the Lord Goring , which was much
increased in number by the addition of those who escaped from
Maidstone , but not in resolution, being so discouraged with their
relation of what had passed there, that, immediately upon our
approach, they began to retreat, many of them returning away to their
own habitations. Notwithstanding this, a considerable body con-
tinuing with the Lord Goring, he sent to the city of London, desiring
leave to march through the city into Essex, designing to recruit his
men with such of that county as had lately expressed so much
affection to the King's interest The city, though much inclined to
have the King received upon terms, yet not willing absolutely to
espouse the cavalier party, especially in a flying posture , and considering, that there was a great number still amongst them who
retained their affection to the public cause, returned a positive denial
to Goring so that he was necessitated to make use of boats, or other
means, to transport his men over the river into the county of Essex
A party of horse was sent from the army to keep a guard at Bow-
bridge, as well to prevent the disaffected in the city from running to
the enemy, as to hinder them from doing anything to the prejudice
of London.

226

Lt-Gen. Cromwel, with that part of the army which was with him, besieged the castle and town of Pembroke, whither the principal of that body which fled from St Faggons had made their retreat   In the mean time the Presbyterian party prevailing in the house, by reason of the absence of divers members who belonged to the army, and were employed in all parts of the nation, discharged from prison those who had been committed upon the account of that force which was put upon the house by the late tumults, and left the parliament to the mercy of their enemies with a very slender guard   The Lord Lisle's commission to be Lord Lieutenant of Ireland expiring at the same time, they refused to renew it : by which means the province of Munster fell into the hands of the Lord Inchiquin, as President; who made use of the opportunity to displace those officers that had been put in by the Lord Lisle, preferring his own creatures to their employ- ments, to the great prejudice of the English interest in that country Many others, who were acquainted with his temper and principles, quitted voluntarily. And though he still pretended fidelity to the state of England, yet he expressed himself dissatisfied with the pro- ceedings of the army-party towards him.   Some overtures also he had received from the ·Irish touching an accommodation   but being straitened by them in his quarters, and therefore advancing with his army towards them, Col Temple, and some others, yet remaining in his army, being willing to improve the occasion, pressed him so hard to resolve to fight, that he could not well avoid it   At the beginning of the battle the success seemed to be very doubtful but in the end ours obtained the victory, some thousands of the enemy being killed, many made prisoners, and all their baggage taken   Not long after this he declared against the parliament, and joined with the Irish rebels Some of the English officers concurred with him in his declaration. Many left him, and came to the parliament, who made provision for them, as they had done for those that came away before   Though this conjunction of Inchiquin was not concluded without the King's consent; yet it was not a proper season for him to condescend so far as they desired whereby great divisions arose amongst them   For there was a party of old Irish, as they were called, headed principally by Owen Roe O Neal, of whom several were in the supreme council, who, out of an innate hatred to the English government, joined with those who would be satisfied with nothing less than to have the Pope acknowledged to be their only supreme lord so that not being able to agree, their differences proved very serviceable to the English interest   The like spirit of division appeared amongst our enemies in Scotland where though the number was great of those that professed their constant adherence to their engagements contained in the covenant , yet when it came to a trial in their convention, the anti covenanters, who were for restoring the King without any terms, carried all before them so that, instead of the Marquis of Argyll, the Marquis of Hamilton was appointed General of their army, all the inferior officers being of the same mold and principle , insomuch, that the pulpits, who before had proclaimed this war, now accompanied the army that was preparing to march with their curses · for though they could have been contented, that the Sectarian party, as they called it, should be ruined, provided they could find strength enough to bring in the King themselves , yet they feared their old enemy more than their new one , because the latter would only restrain them from lording it over them and others, affording them equal liberty with themselves whereas the former was so far from that, as hardly to suffer them to be hewers of wood and drawers of water , for those who would have all power, both civil and ecclesiastical, put into one hand, could not possibly agree with such as would have it divided into many.

These affairs necessitated the parliament to raise the militia, in order to oppose this malevolent spirit which threatened them fiom the north , and also prevailed with them to discountenance a charge of high treason, framed by Maj Huntington, an officer of the army, with the advice of some members of both houses, against Lt-Gen· Cromwel, for endeavouring, by betraying the King, parliament and army, to advance himself, it being manifest, that the preferring this accusation at that time, was principally designed to take him off from his command, and thereby to weaken the army, that their enemies might be the better enabled to prevail against them

The design of the King's escape was still carried on , but, by the vigilance of the Governor of the Isle of Wight, and his officers, it was discovered and prevented   The next morning after the discovery, they found the iron bars of the King's chamber-window eaten through

by something applied to them   Whereupon those who were to have
been instrumental in his escape, not knowing otherwise how to
revenge themselves on those who had defeated their enterprize,
accused Maj Rolfe, a Captain in that garrison, very active and vigi-
lant in his charge, of a design to kill the King, raising such a
clamour about it, that the parliament thought not fit to decline the
putting him upon his trial but the accusation appearing to the grand
jury to be grounded upon malice, they refused to find the bill
About the same time Capt Burleigh, who had beat a drum at Newport
for the rescuing of the King, was brought to his trial, and the jury
having found him guilty of high treason, he was executed according
to the sentence.

Those of the enemy commanded by the Lord Goring who had
fled into Essex, grew to a considerable number but being new-raised
men, and not well acquainted one with another, upon the advance of
our army retreated to Colchester, with a body so much exceeding
ours, which pursued and besieged them in that place, that Commissary-General Ireton compared the town, and those therein, to a great
bee hive, and our army to a small swarm of bees sticking on one side
of it   But the number of ours was soon increased by the forces
which the well affected in the counties of Essex, Suffolk, Norfolk,
and Cambridge, sent to their assistance

The Earl of Holland, who at the beginning of the parliament had
appeared active for them, and afterwards leaving them, had gone to
the King at Oxford, when he supposed him to grow strong, then
again returning to the parliament upon the declining of the King's
affairs, publishing a declaration at his coming to London, that he
left the King because he saw the Irish rebels so eminently favoured
by him, in this low condition of the parliament, revolted again, and
formed a party of 1000 horse, with which he marched from London,
and declared against them, accompanied by the Duke of Buckingham, (whose sequestration, upon the account of his minority when
he first engaged with the King, the parliament had freely remitted),
and the Lord Francis his brother, prevailing also with Dalbier,
formerly Quartermaster-General to the Earl of Essex, to join with
them.   Their rendezvous was appointed to be upon Bansted downs

But the vigilance of the parliament was such, that a party of horse and foot was soon sent after them, commanded by Sir Michael Lewesey, who without much dispute put those courtly Gentlemen to the rout. The Lord Francis, presuming perhaps that his beauty would have charmed the soldiers, as it had done Mis Kirk, for whom he had made a splendid entertainment the night before he left the town, and made her a present of plate to the value of £1000, staid behind his company, where, unseasonably daring the troopers, and refusing to take quarter, he was killed, and after his death there was found upon him some of the hair of Mrs Kirk sewed in a piece of ribbon that hung next his skin The rest fled towards St Neots, in the county of Huntington, where, being fallen upon again, they were routed a second time in which action the parliament's soldiers, to express their detestation of Dalbeir's treachery, hewed him in pieces The Earl of Holland was taken, and sent prisoner to Warwick castle but the Duke of Buckingham escaped, and went over to France.

Pomfret castle being seized by some of the King's party, was besieged by the country, assisted by some of the army, Sir Hugh Cholmondeley commanding at the siege But the army, finding little progress made therein, ordered Col Rainsborough with more forces thither appointing him to command in the room of Sir Hugh Cholmondeley Whilst he was preparing for that service, being at Doncaster, ten or twelve miles from Pomfret, with a considerable force in the town, a party of horse dismounting at his quarters, and going up as friends to his chamber, under pretence of having business with him, seized him first, and, upon his refusal to go silently with them, murdered him After his death, another commander being appointed in his place to carry on the siege, those in the castle were reduced to such extremities, that some of the most desperate of them resolved, together with their Governor one Morris, who had been page to the Earl of Strafford, to endeavour the breaking, through our forces on horseback which they attempted And though most of them were beaten back to the castle by the besiegers, yet this Morris made his way through, but was afterwards taken as he passed through the country in the disguise of a beggar, and

230

carried to York, where he was arraigned before Justice Thorpe, and being found guilty of treason, was executed for the same

Lt-Gen. Cromwel. with that part of the army which was with him, besieged the town and castle of Pembroke , whither the chief of that party that fled from St. Faggons had made their retreat, as I said before but wanting great guns, he was obliged to send for some to Gloucester, which with much difficulty were brought to him   This place detained the greatest part of our army about six weeks   But it was remarkable, that about the time the Scots were entering into England, the garrison, for want of provisions, was forced to capitulate and surrender upon articles , by which some of them were to remain prisoners, and others to be banished into Ireland for three years. Amongst the latter were Col Thomas Stradling, Sir Henry Stradling, Col Button, and Maj Butler , of the first were, Col Laughern. Col Poyer, and Col. Powell.

Twenty thousand Scots being upon their march into England under the conduct of Duke Hamilton, with about 5000 English commanded by Sir Marmaduke Langdale , some of us who had opposed the Lieutenant-General's arbitrary proceedings when we were convinced he acted to promote a selfish and unwarrantable design, now thinking ourselves obliged to strengthen his hands in that necessary work which he was appointed to undertake, writ a letter to him, to encourage him, from the consideration of the justice of the cause wherein he was engaged, and the wickedness of those with whom he was to encounter, to proceed with chearfulness , assuring him, that, notwithstanding all our discouragements, we would readily give him all the assistance we could.   The house of Commons declared the Scots who had invaded England to be enemies, and ordered the Lieutenant-General to advance towards them, and fight them   But the Lords, in this doubtful posture of affairs, declined to concur with them in the same   Yet both of them, with the city of London, joined in driving on a personal treaty with the King in the Isle of Wight , and to that end the Lords and Commons revoked the votes for non-addresses , whereby the King seemed to be on sure ground , for that if the Scots army failed, he might still make terms with the parliament.   The King's party in Colchester were also much encour-

231

aged with hopes of relief from the Scots army, who were very numerous, and well furnished with all things but a good cause   To fight
this formidable army, the Lieutenant-General could not make up
much above 7000 horse and foot, and those so extremely harrassed
with hard service and long marches, that they seemed rather fit for a
hospital than a battle   With this handful of men he advanced
towards the enemy, and about Preston in Lancashire both armies
met on the 17th of August 1648   The English who were in the
Scots army, had the honour of the van, and for a time entertained
ours with some opposition, but being vigorously pressed by our men,
they were forced to retreat to a pass, which they maintained against
us, whilst they sent to their General for succours, which he not
sending, on purpose, as was said, that the English might be cut off, and
his party kept entire to enable him to set up for himself, and give law to
both nations, they began to shift for themselves   which made such an
impression upon the Scots, that they soon followed their example,
retreating in a disorderly manner.   Ours followed them so close,
that most of their foot threw down their arms, and yielded themselves prisoners   Many of the principal officers of their foot were
taken, with all their artillery, ammunition, and baggage   Hamilton,
with 4 or 5000 horse in a body, left the field, and was pursued by
Col Thorney, a member of parliament, and Colonel of a regiment of
horse, a worthy and valiant man, who following them too close and
unadvisedly, run himself upon one of their lances, wherewith he was
mortally wounded, which he perceiving by the wasting of his spirits, to
express his affection to his country, and joy for the defeat of the
enemy, desired his men to open to the right and left, that he might
have the satisfaction to see them run before he died.   The enemy's
body of horse kept themselves together for some days, roving up and
down the country about Leicestershire, which county the Lord Grey
of Grooby had raised, and brought together about 3000 horse and
foot to preserve the country from plunder, and to take all possible
advantages against the enemy   And tho' a body of horse from the
army was in pursuit of the Scots, yet the Leicestershire party came
up first to them at Uttoxeter in Staffordshire, where the body of
the enemy's horse was, and whilst the Scots were treating with the
other party from the army, the Lord Grey's men observing no guards
kept, entered upon them before any conditions were made, where-
232

upon Hamilton surrendered himself to Col. Wayte, an officer of the Leicestershire party, delivering to him his scarf, his George, and his sword, which last he desired him to keep carefully, because it had belonged to his ancestors. By the two parties the Scots were all made prisoners, and all their horses seized. The Duke of Hamilton was carried prisoner to Windsor castle, and all their standards of horse and foot were taken, and sent up to London, where the parliament ordered them to be hung up in Wesminster-hall. The house of Lords who had avoided to declare the Scots enemies whilst their army was entire, now after their defeat prevented the house of Commons, and moved that a day might be appointed to give God thanks for this success. The news of this victory being carried to the Isle of Wight, the King said to the Governor, that it was the worst news that ever came to England: to which he answered, That he thought the King had no cause to be of that opinion, since if Hamilton had beaten the English, he would certainly have possessed himself of the thrones of England and Scotland. The King presently replied, "You are mistaken, I could have commanded him back with "the motion of my hand." Which whether he could do or no, was doubtful; but whatever reasons he had for this opinion, it seemed very unseasonable to own it openly in that conjuncture. Lt.-Gen. Cromwel marched with part of his army to Edinburgh, where he dispossessed the Hamiltonian party of their authority, and put the power into the hands of the Presbyterians, by whom he was received with great demonstrations of joy. And tho' lately they looked upon the Independent party as the worst of their enemies, yet now they owned and embraced them as their best friends and deliverers, and having notice given them, that the English army was about to return into England, they prevailed with the Lieutenant-General to leave Maj.-Gen Lambert with a body of horse, till they could raise more forces to provide for their own safety.

The treaty with the King being pressed with more heat than ever, and a design visibly appearing to render all our victories useless thereby, by the advice of some friends I went down to the army, which lay at that time before Colchester: where attending upon the General, Sir Thomas Fairfax, to acquaint him with the state of affairs at London, I told him, that a design was driving on to betray the

cause in which so much of the people's blood had been shed, that
the King being under a restraint, would not account himself obliged
by anything he should promise under such circumstances, assuring
him, that most of those who pushed on the treaty with the greatest
vehemency, intended not that he should be bound to the performance
of it, but designed principally to use his authority and favour in
order to destroy the army, who, as they had assumed the power,
ought to make the best use of it, and to prevent the ruin of themselves and the nation   He acknowledged what I said to be true,
and declared himself resolved to use the power he had, to maintain
the cause of the public, upon a clear and evident call, looking upon
himself to be obliged to pursue the work which he was about   Perceiving by such a general answer that he was irresolute, I went to
Commissary-General Ireton, who had a great influence upon him, and
having found him, we discoursed together upon the same subject,
wherein we both agreed that it was necessary for the army to inter-
pose in this matter. but differed about the time, he being of opinion,
that it was to permit the King and the parliament to make an agreement, and to wait till they had made a full discovery of their intentions, whereby the people becoming sensible of their own danger,
would willingly join to oppose them   My opinion was, that it would
be much easier for the army to keep them from a conjunction, than
to oppose them when united, it being highly probable, that the first
things they would fall upon after their union, would be such as were
most taking with the people, in order to oblige them to assist in the
disbanding of the army, under pretence of lessening their taxes   and
then if the army should in any manner signify a dislike of their proceedings, they would be esteemed by the majority of the people, to
be disturbers of the public peace, and accused of designing nothing
save their own particular advantages.

The King's party in Colchester expecting to be included in the
peace which was treating between him and the parliament, held out
to the utmost, but being in extreme want of provisions, and destitute
of all hopes of relief since the defeat of the Scots, they were forced
to surrender, on the 28th of August 1648, upon articles, whereby
some of the principal of them being prisoners at discretion, the court-
martial assembled, and condemned Sir Charles Lucas, Sir George

234

Lisle, and Sir Barnard Gascoin, to die, the last of whom being a foreigner, was pardoned, and the other two were shot to death according to the sentence The Lord Goring and the Lord Capel were sent prisoners to London, and committed to the Tower by an order of the parliament

The two houses finding things in this posture, hastened the departure of their commissioners to the Isle of Wight, with powers and instructions to treat with the King, who principally insisted on that article concerning Bishops, whom he accounted to be by divine right, or rather essentially necessary to the support of arbitrary power Whereupon Ministers of each side were appointed to dispute touching that subject, in order to satisfy the King's conscience But the army having now wonderfully dispersed their enemies on every part, began to consider how to secure themselves and the common cause against the councils that were carried on in opposition to them, under pretext of making peace with the King, and to that end drew up a declaration at St Alban's, dated the 16th of November 1648, shewing, That the grounds of their first engagement was, to bring delinquents to justice, that the King was guilty of the blood shed in the first and second war, and that therefore they could not trust him with the government This remonstrance they presented to the parliament on the 20th of November 1648 The King and parliament, seeing this cloud beginning to gather, endeavoured by all means possible to hasten their treaty to a conclusion The army also were not wanting to fortify themselves against that shock, sending some of their own number to those members of parliament whom they esteemed most faithful to the common cause, to invite them down to the army, after they should in a public manner have expressed their dissatisfaction to the proceedings of those who had betrayed the trust reposed in them by the good people of England, and declared, that finding it impossible to be any farther serviceable in parliament, they had resolved to repair to the army, in order to procure their assistance in settling the government of the nation upon a just foundation At a meeting of some members of parliament with the said officers from the army, it was resolved, That though the way proposed by them might be taken in case all other means failed, yet, seeing there was more than a sufficient number of members in the parliament to make

235

a house, who were most affectionate to the public cause, it would be more proper for the army to relieve them from those who rendered them useless to the public service, thereby preserving the name and place of the parliament, than for the members thereof to quit their stations wherein they were appointed to serve, and to leave the civil authority in the hands of those who would be ready to fall in with any power that would attempt to frustrate what should be agreed on by them and the army In prosecution of this result, the army drew to Colebrook, from whence Commissary-General Ireton sent me word, that now he hoped they should please me which I must acknowledge they did by the way which they were taking, not from any particular advantages that I expected from it, except an equal share of security with other men, but that the people of England might be preserved in their just rights, from the oppressions of violent men, the question in dispute between the King's party and us being, as I apprehended, ' Whether the King should govern as a god by his " will, and the nation be governed by force like beasts ? or, Whether " the people should be governed by laws made by themselves, and " live under a government derived from their own consent?" being fully persuaded, that an accommodation with the King was unsafe to the people of England, and unjust and wicked in the nature of it The former, besides that it was obvious to all men, the King himself had proved, by the duplicity of his dealing with the parliament, which manifestly appeared in his own papers taken at the battle of Naseby, and elsewhere Of the latter I was convinced by the express words of God's Law " That blood defileth the land, and the land " cannot be cleansed of the blood that is shed therein, but by the " blood of him that shed it." *Numb* xxxv 33 And therefore I could not consent to the counsels of those who were contented to leave the guilt of so much blood upon the nation, and thereby to draw down the just vengeance of God upon us all, when it was most evident, that the war had been occasioned by the invasion of our rights, and open breach of our laws and constitution on the King's part

The commissioners that were appointed to manage the treaty with the King, returned with the King's answer, containing neither a positive grant, nor an absolute denial As to the Bishops, he still retained his principle of their divine right, and therefore declared

236

that he could not dispense with the abolition of them : but for present satisfaction, hoping by giving ground, to gain a better opportunity to serve them, he consented, that those who had bought their lands, should have a lease of them for some years and for satisfaction for the blood that had been shed, he was willing that six should be excepted , but withal care was taken, that they should be such as were far enough from the reach of justice By another article, the militia was to remain in the parliament for ten years . thereby implying, if I mistake not, that the right of granting it was in the King, and consequently that we had done him wrong in contending with him for it. By such ways and means did some men endeavour to abuse the nation

Some of our commissioners who had been with the King, pleaded in the house for a concurrence with him, as if they had been employed by him , though others with more ingenuity acknowledged, that they would not advise an agreement upon those terms, were it not to prevent a greater evil that was like to ensue upon the refusal of them   But Sir Henry Vane so truly stated the matter of fact relating to the treaty, and so evidently discovered the design and deceit of the King's answer, that he made it clear to us, that by it the justice of our cause was not asserted, nor our rights secured for the future , concluding, that if they should accept of these terms without the concurrence of the army, it would prove but a feather in their caps. Notwithstanding which, the corrupt party in the house, having bargained for their own and the nation's liberty, resolved to break through all hazards and inconveniences to make good their contract, and, after twenty four hours debate, resolved by the plurality of votes, "That the King's concessions were ground for a future "settlement" At which some of us expressing our dissatisfaction, desired that our protestation might be entered   But that being denied, as against the orders of the house, I contented myself to declare publicly, that, being convinced that they had deserted the common cause and interest of the nation, I could no longer join with them , the rest of those who dissented, also expressing themselves much to the same purpose. The day following, some of the principal officers of the army came to London, with expectation that things would be brought to this issue. And consulting with some

members of parliament and others, it was concluded, after a full and
free debate, That the measures taken by the parliament were contrary to the trust reposed in them, and tending to contract the guilt
of the blood that had been shed, upon themselves and the nation .
that it was therefore the duty of the army, to endeavour to put a
stop to such proceedings , having engaged in the war, not simply as
mercenaries, but out of judgment and conscience, being convinced
that the cause in which they were engaged was just, and that
the good of the people was involved in it Being come to this
resolution, three of the members of the house, and three of the
officers of the army, withdrew into a private room, to consider of the
best means to attain the ends of our said resolution , where we agreed,
That the army should be drawn up the next morning, and guards
placed in Westminster-hall, the court of requests, and the lobby, that
none might be permitted to pass into the house but such as had continued faithful to the public interest To this end, we went over the
names of all the members one by one, giving the truest characters
we could of their inclinations , wherein I presume we were not
mistaken in many For the parliament was fallen into such factions
and divisions, that any one who usually attended and observed the
business of the house, could, after a debate upon any question,
easily number the votes that would be on each side, before the question was put Commissary-General Ireton went to Sir Thomas Fairfax, and acquainted him with the necessity of this extraordinary way
of proceeding having taken care to have the army drawn up the
next morning by seven of the clock Col Pride commanded the
guard that attended at the parliament-doors, having a list of those
members who were to be excluded , preventing them from entering
into the house, and securing some of the most suspected under a
guard provided for that end , in which he was assisted by the Lord
Grey of Grooby and others, who knew the members To justify these
proceedings, the army sent a message to the house, representing,
That whereas divers members had been expelled the house upon
account of the violence done to the parliament by the city of London
and others, in 1647 , yet, upon the absence of many well-affected
members, by reason of their employments in the army and elsewhere
against the enemy, the said persons were readmitted without any trial
or satisfaction in the things whereof they were accused , whereby the
238

Scots had been drawn to invade this kingdom, and the house prevented by the intruders and their accomplices from declaring against
the invaders, who had made up the number of ninety odd votes to
that purpose · and whereas, by the prevalency of the same corrupt
councils, justice had been obstructed, and a settlement of affairs
hindered and, lastly, the King's concessions declared to be a ground
for the settlement of peace, notwithstanding the insufficiency and
defects of them they therefore most humbly desired, that all those
members who are innocent in these things, would by a public declaration acquit themselves from any guilt thereof, or concurrence therein ,
and that those who shall not so acquit themselves, may be excluded
or suspended the house till they have given clear satisfaction therein ,
that those who have faithfully performed their trust, may proceed
without interruption to the execution of justice , and to make speedy
provision for an equal succession of representatives, wherein differences may be composed, and all men comfortably acquiesce as they
for their parts thereby engaged and assured them they would. The
house, wherein there was about six score, was moved to send for
those members who were thus excluded by the army , which they did,
as I presume, rather upon the account of decency, than from any
desire they had that their message should be obeyed , and that it
might clearly appear, that this interruption proceeded from the army,
and not from any advice of the parliament , to the end that what they
should act separately, might be esteemed to be only in order to prevent such inconveniences as might otherwise fall upon the nation, if
the whole power should be left in the hands of an army , and that
their actions appearing to be founded upon this necessity, they might
the better secure the respect and obedience of the people Upon
such considerations, when the Serjeant returned, and acquainted
them, that the excluded members were detained by the army, the
house proceeded in the business before them

Lt-Gen Cromwel the night after the interruption of the house
arrived from Scotland, and lay at Whitehall , where, and at other
places, he declared that he had not been acquainted with this design,
yet since it was done, he was glad of it, and would endeavour to
maintain it

Maj. Gen. Harrison being sent by the army with a party of horse

239

to bring the King from the Isle of Wight, Col Hammond, who was intrusted with the custody of him by the parliament, disputed to deliver him, but finding that those about him inclined to comply, he thought it not convenient to make any farther opposition So that the King was conducted from the island to Hurst Castle, and from thence to Windsor, by Maj.-Gen. Harrison Being on his way, he dined at Mr. Leviston's in Bagshot park, who had provided a horse for him to make his escape but this design also was discovered, and prevented The King being at Windsor, it was debated what should be done with him The army were for bringing him to a trial, for levying war against the parliament and people of England, and the common council of the city of London presented a petition to the parliament, by the hands of Col Titchburn, to that effect But some of the commonwealth's men desired, that before they consented to that method, it might be resolved what government to establish, fearing a design in the army to set up some one of themselves in his room Others endeavoured to persuade them, that the execution of justice ought to be their first work, in respect of their duty to God and the people, that the failure therein had been already the occasion of a second war, which was justly to be charged on the parliament for neglecting that duty, that those who were truly commonwealth's men, ought to be of that opinion, as the most probable means to obtain their desires in the establishment of an equal and just government ; and that the officers of the army, who were chiefly to be suspected, could not be guilty of so much impudence and folly, to erect an arbitrary power in any one of themselves, after they had in so public a manner declared their detestation of it in another

In order to the accomplishment of the important work which the house of Commons had now before them, they voted, "That by the "fundamental laws of the land, it is treason for the King of England "for the time being, to levy war against the parliament and kingdom." To which the Lords not concurring, they passed it the next day without their consent, and the day after declared, "That the people are, "under God, the original of all just power, that the house of Com- "mons, being chosen by, and representing the people, are the "supreme power in the nation; that whatsoever is enacted or declared

" for law by the Commons in parliament, hath the force of a law,
" and the people are concluded thereby, though the consent of King
" or Peers be not had thereto "

This obstruction being removed, several petitions were brought to
the parliament, for so the house of Commons now styled themselves,
from the city of London, borough of Southwark, and most of the
counties in England, requesting that the King might be brought to
justice   in order to which, they passed an act, authorising the
persons therein named, or any thirty of them, to proceed to the
arraignment, condemnation or acquittal of the King, with full power,
in case of condemnation, to proceed to sentence, and to cause the
said sentence to be put in execution

This high court of justice met on the 8th of January 1648, in the
Painted chamber, to the number of about fourscore, consisting chiefly
of members of Parliament, officers of the army, and gentlemen of the
country, where they chose Serjeant Aske, Serjeant Steel, and Dr.
Dorrislaus, to be their counsel, Mr John Coke of Gray's-Inn to be
their Solicitor, and Mr Andrew Broughton their Secretary, and sent
out a precept, under their hands and seals, for proclaiming the court
to be held in Westminster-hall on the 10th of the said month, which
was performed accordingly by Serjeant Dendy, attended by a party
of horse, in Cheapside, before the Old Exchange, and in Westminster-
hall.   On the 10th, they chose Serjeant Bradshaw to be their President, with Mr. Lisle and Mr Say to be his assistants.   And a charge
of high treason being drawn up against the King, the court appointed
a convenient place to be prepared at the upper end of Westminster-
hall for his public trial, directing it to be covered with scarlet cloth,
and ordered twenty halberdiers to attend the President, and thirty
the King.

All things being thus prepared for the trial, the King was conducted from Windsor to St James's   From whence, on the 20th of
January, he was brought to the bar of the high court of justice,
where the President acquainted the King with the causes of his
being brought to that place : for that he, contrary to the trust
reposed in him by the people, to see the laws put in execution for

241

their good, had made use of his power to subvert those laws, and to set up his will and pleasure as a law over them · that, in order to effect that design, he had endeavoured the suppression of parliaments, the best defence of the people's liberties that he had levied war against the parliament and people of England, wherein great numbers of the good people had been slain , of which blood the parliament presuming him guilty, had appointed this high court of justice for the trial of him for the same Then turning to Mr Broughton, clerk of the court, he commanded him to read the charge against the King , who, as the clerk was reading the charge, interrupted him, saying, " I am not intrusted by the people, they are " mine by inheritance ," demanding by what authority they brought him thither The President answered, That they derived their authority from an act made by the Commons of England assembled in parliament The King said, The Commons could not give an oath , that they were no court, and therefore could make no act for the trial of any man, much less of him their sovereign It was replied, That the Commons assembled in parliament could acknowledge no other sovereign but God , for that upon his and the people's appeal to the sword for the decision of their respective pretensions, judgment had been given for the people , who, conceiving it to be their duty not to bear the sword in vain, had appointed the court to make inquisition for the blood that had been shed in that dispute Whereupon the President, being moved by Mr Solicitor Coke, in the name, and on the behalf of the good people of England, commanded the clerk of the court to proceed in the reading of the charge against him Which being done, the King was required to give his answer to it, and to plead Guilty or Not guilty The King demurred to the jurisdiction of the court , affirming that no man, nor body of men, had power to call him to an account, being not intrusted by man, and therefore accountable only to God for his actions , entering upon a large discourse of his being in treaty with the parliament's commissioners at the Isle of Wight, and his being taken from thence he knew not how, when he thought he was come to a conclusion with them This discourse seeming not to the purpose, the President told him, that as to his plea of not being accountable to man, seeing God, by his providence, had over-ruled it, the court had resolved to do so also , and that if he would give no other

242

answer, that which he had given should be registered, and they would proceed as if he had confessed the charge   In order to which, the President commanded his answer to be entered, directing Serjeant Dendy, who attended the court, to withdraw the prisoner, which, as he was doing, many persons cried out in the hall, *Justice, 'Justice*   The King being withdrawn, the court adjourned into the Painted chamber, to consider what farther was fit to be done, and being desirous to prevent all objections tending to accuse them of haste or surprise, they resolved to conveen him before them publicly twice more   after which, if he persisted in his demurrer to the jurisdiction of the court then to give judgment against him   And that nothing might be wanting, in case he should resolve to plead, they appointed witnesses to be examined to every article of the charge   At the King's second appearance before the court, which was on the 22nd of January, he carried himself in the same manner as before   Whereupon his refusal being again entered, and he withdrawn, the court adjourned to the Painted chamber   On the 23d of January, the King was brought a third time before the commissioners, where refusing to plead, as he had done before, his refusal was entered, and witnesses examined publicly, to prove the charge of his levying war against the parliament   After which, Solicitor-General Coke demanded of the court, that they would proceed to the pronouncing of sentence against the prisoner at the bar   Whereupon the court adjourned into the Painted chamber, and upon serious consideration, declared the King to be a tyrant, traitor, murderer, and a public enemy to the commonwealth   that his condemnation extend unto death, by severing his head from his body, and that a sentence grounded upon those votes be prepared, which being agreed upon, the King should be ordered on the next day following to receive it   The sentence being ingrossed, was read on the 27th of January   and thereupon the court resolved, That the same should be the sentence, which should be read and published in Westminster-hall the same day, that the President should not permit the King to speak after the sentence pronounced, that he should openly declare it to be the sense and judgment of the court, and that the commissioners should signify their consent by standing up   In the afternoon, the King was brought to the bar, and desired that he might be permitted to make one proposition before they proceeded to sentence, which he

243

earnestly pressing, as that which he thought would tend to the reconciling of all parties, and to the peace of the three kingdoms, they permitted him to offer it The effect of which was, that he might meet the two houses in the Painted chamber, to whom he doubted not to offer that which should satisfy and secure all interests, designing, as I have been since informed, to propose his own resignation, and the admission of his son to the throne, upon such terms as should have been agreed upon This motion being new and unexpected to the court, who were not willing to deny or grant any thing without serious deliberation, they withdrew to consider of it into the inner court of wards and being satisfied, upon debate, that nothing but loss of time would be the consequence of it, they returned into the court with a negative to his demand ; telling him, That they met there as a court of justice, commissionated by the parliament, of whose authority they were fully satisfied that, by their commission, they were not authorised to receive any proposals from him, but to proceed to the trial of him that, in order thereto, his charge had been read to him , to which, if he would have pleaded, the counsel for the commonwealth were ready to have proved it against him · that he had thrice demurred to the jurisdiction of the court , which demurrer the court had over-ruled, and registered , ordering to pro ceed against him, as if he had confessed the charge and that if he had any proposition to make, it was proper for him to address it to the parliament, and not to them Then the President enlarged upon the horrid nature of those crimes of which he had been accused, and was now convicted , declaring, That the only just power of Kings was derived from the consent of the people that whereas the people had intrusted him to see their laws put in execution, he had endeavoured, throughout the whole course of his reign, to subvert those good laws, and to introduce an arbitrary and tyrannical government in the room of them that, to cut off all hopes of redress, he had attempted, from the beginning of his reign, either wholly to destroy parliaments, or to render them only subservient to his own corrupt designs that though he had consented, the public necessities so requiring, that this parliament should not be dissolved but by an act of themselves, he had levied war against them, that he might not only dissolve them, but, by the terror of his power, for ever discourage such assemblies from doing their duty that in this war many thousands of the good people

of England had lost their lives· that, in obedience to what God
commanded, and the nation expected, the parliament had appointed
this court to make inquisition for this blood, and to try him for the
same that his charge had been read to him, and he required to give
an answer to it, which he having thrice refused to do, he acquainted
him, that the court had resolved to pronounce sentence against him,
and thereupon commanded the clerk to read it, which he did, being
to this effect THAT THE KING, FOR THE CRIMES CONTAINED IN THE
CHARGE, SHOULD BE CARRIED BACK TO THE PLACE FROM WHENCE HE
CAME, AND THENCE TO THE PLACE OF EXECUTION, WHERE HIS HEAD
SHOULD BE SEVERED FROM HIS BODY Which sentence being read,
the commisssioners testified their unanimous assent by their standing
up The King would have spoken something before he was withdrawn, but being accounted dead in law immediately after sentence
pronounced, it was not permitted. The court withdrew also, and
agreed, that the sentence should be put in execution on the Tuesday
following, which would be the 30th of January 1648. The King,
having refused such Ministers as the court appointed to attend him,
desired that Dr Juxton, late Bishop of London, might be permitted
to come to him, which being granted, and Adjutant-General Allen
sent to acquaint the Doctor with the King's condition and desires,
he, being altogether unprepared for such a work, broke out into these
expressions, "God save me, what a trick is this, that I should have
"no more warning, and I have nothing ready!" but, recollecting
himself a little, he put on his scarf, and his other furniture, and went
with him to the King, where, having read the common-prayer, and
one of his old sermons, he administered the sacrament to him, not
forgetting to use the words of the confession set down in the liturgy,
inviting all those that truly repent to make their confession before the
congregation then gathered together, though there was none present
but the King and himself

The high court of justice appointed a committee to inspect the
parts about Whitehall for a convenient place for the execution of the
King, who having made their report, it was agreed, that a scaffold
should be erected to that purpose near the Banqueting-house, and
order given to cover it with black The same day, being the 29th of
January, they signed a warrant for his execution, to which about

threescore of the commissioners set their hands and seals ; directing
it to Col. Hacker, Col Hunks, and Col Phaier, or either of them
The Duke of Gloucester and the Lady Elisabeth waited on the
King the same day to take their leave of him   An Extraordinary
Ambassador from the United Provinces had his audience in the
parliament.   His business was, to interceed with them for the life of
the King, and to preserve a fair correspondence between England
and the States.   The next day, about eight in the morning, the King,
attended by a guard, was brought from S James's, through the park,
to Whitehall, where, having drunk a glass or two of iced wine, and
staid about two hours in a private room, he was conducted to the
scaffold out of a window of the Banqueting-house, and having made
a speech, and taken off his George, he kneeled down at the block,
and the executioner performed his office   The body was ordered to
be interred at Windsor   The Duke of Lennox, the Marquis of Hert-
ford, the Earls of Southampton and Lindsey, with some others,
having leave from the parliament, attended it to the grave

APPENDIX I.

Propositions delivered to his MAJESTY

BY THE

Earl of Strafford,

For SECURING of his MAJESTY'S ESTATE,

And BRIDLING of PARLIAMENTS,

And for increase of his revenue much more than it is.

TOuching the first, having considered divers means, I find none so important to strengthen your Majesty's Regal authorities against all oppositions or practices of troublesome spirits, as to fortify your kingdom, by having a fortress in every chief town and important place thereof, furnished with ordnance, munition, and faithful men, as they ought to be, with all other circumstances fit to be digested in a business of this nature

Ordering withal the trained soldiers of the country to be united in one dependency with the said forts, as well to secure their beginnings, as to secure them in any occasion of suspect, and keep their arms for more security, whereby the countries are no less to be brought into subjection than the cities themselves, and consequently the whole kingdom, your Majesty having, by this course, the power thereof in your own hands

The reasons of these suggestions.

First, That, in policy, it is a greater tye of the people by force and necessity, than merely by love and affection for by the one the government resteth always secure, but by the other, no longer than the people are well contented.

Secondly, It forceth obstinate subjects to be no more presumptuous than it pleaseth your Majesty to permit them

249

Thirdly, That to have a state unfurnished, is to give the bridle thereof to the subject, when by the contrary it resteth only in the prince's hand

Fourthly, That modern fortresses take long time in winning, with such charge and difficulty as no subjects in these times have means probable to attempt them

Fifthly, That it is a sure remedy against rebellious and popular mutinies, or against foreign powers ; because they cannot well succeed, when by this course the apparent means is taken away, to force the King and state upon a doubtful fortune of a set battle, as was the cause that moved the pretended invasion against the land attempted by the King of Spain, 1588

Sixthly, That your Majesty's government is now secured by the people's more subjection, and by their subjection your parliament must be forced consequently to alter their style, and to be conform-able to your will and pleasure   for their words and opposition importeth nothing, where the power is in your Majesty's own hands, to do with them what you please , being indeed the chief purpose of this discourse, and the secret intent thereof, fit to be concealed from any English at all, either counsellor of state or others

For these and other weighty reasons, it may be considered in this place, to make your Majesty more powerful and strong, some orders be observed, that are used in fortified countries, the government thereof importeth as much as the states themselves, I mean in times of doubt and suspect, which are these.

Imprimis, That none wear arms or weapons at all, either in city or country, but such as your Majesty may think fit to privilege , and they to be inrolled

Secondly, That as many high-ways as conveniently may be done, may be made passable through those cities and towns fortified, to constrain the passengers to travel through them.

Thirdly, That soldiers of fortresses be sometimes chosen of another nation, if subjects to the same prince , but howsoever not to be born in the same province, or within forty miles of the fortress , and not to have friends or correspondency near it.

250

Fourthly, That at the gates of such walled towns be appointed officers, not to suffer any unknown passenger to pass without a ticket, shewing from whence he came, and whither he goeth ; and that the gates of each city be shut at night, and the keys be kept by the Mayor or Governor Also that the inn-keepers do deliver the names of all unknown passengers that lodge in their houses , and if they stay suspiciously at any time, to present them to the Governor : whereby dangerous persons seeing these strict courses, will be more wary of their actions, and thereby mischievous attempts will be prevented All which being referred to your Majesty's wise consideration, it is meet for me withal to give you some satisfaction of the charge and time to perform what is proposed, that you may not be discouraged in the difficulty of the one, or prolongation of the other. Both which doubts are resolved in one and the same reason , in respect that in England each chief town commonly hath a ruinated castle, well seated for strength whose foundation and stone remaining, may be both quickly repaired for this use, and with little charge , and made strong enough, I hope, for this purpose in the space of one year, by adding withal bulwarks and rampiers, according to the rules of fortification.

The ordnance for these forts may be of iron , and not to disfurnish your Majesty's navy, or be at a greater charge than is needful to maintain yearly the forts

I make account, in ordinary pay, three thousand men will be sufficient , and will require forty thousand pounds charge *per annum*, or thereabouts, being an expence that inferior princes undergo for their necessary safety All which prevention added to the invincible sea-forces your Majesty hath already, and may have, will make you the most powerful and obeyed prince of the world , which I could likewise confirm by many examples, but I omit them for brevity, and not to confuse your Majesty with too much matter Your gracious Majesty may find, by the scope of this discourse, the means shewed in general to bridle your subjects, that may either be discontented or obstinate So likewise am I to conclude the same intent, particularly against the perverseness of your parliament, as well to suppress that pernicious humour, as to avoid their oppositions against your profit , being the second part to be discoursed on

251

And therefore have first thought fit, for better prevention thereof, to make known to your Majesty the purpose of a general oath your subjects may take, for sure avoiding of all rubs that may hinder the conclusion of those businesses

It is further meant, that no subject upon pain of high treason may refuse the same oath, containing only matter of allegiance, and not scruples or points of conscience, that may gain pretence to be denied.

The effect of the oath is this

THat all your Majesty's subjects do acknowledge you to be *absolute King and Monarch* within your dominions, as is among the Christian princes, and your prerogative as great, whereby you may and shall* of yourself by your Majesty's proclamation, as well as any other sovereign princes doing the like, make laws, or reverse any made, with any other act so great a monarch as yourself may do, and that without further consent of parliaments, or need to call them at all in such cases, confirming, that the parliament in all matters (excepting causes to be sentenced at the high court) ought to be subject unto your Majesty's will, to give the negative or affirmative conclusion, and not to be constrained by their impertinences to any inconvenience, appertaining to your Majesty's Royal authority, and this notwithstanding any bad pretence or custom to the contrary in practice, which (indeed) were fitter to be offered a prince elected without any other right, than to your Majesty, born successively King of England, Scotland, and Ireland, and your heirs for ever, and so resumed, not only of your subjects, but also of the whole world. How necessary the dangerous supremacy of parliament-usurpation is to be prevented, the example of Lewis XI King of France doth manifest, who found the like opposition as your Majesty doth, and by his wisdom suppressed it, and that to the purpose here intended · which is not to put down altogether parliaments, and their authority, being in many cases very necessary and fit, but to abridge them, so far as they seek to derogate from your Majesty's Royal authority, or advancement of your greatness.

The caution in offering the aforesaid oath may require some policy, for the easier passage of it at first, either by singular or particular tractation, and that so near at one time over the land, as one government may not know what the other intendeth, so it may pass the easier by having no time of combination or opposition

There is another means also more certain than this, to bring to pass this oath more easily, as also your profit, and what is pretended, which here I omit for brevity, requiring a long discourse by itself, and have set it down in particular instructions to inform your Majesty.

The second part of this discourse, is touching your Majesty's profit, after your state is secured wherein I shall observe both some reasonable content to the people, as also consider the great expences that princes have now-a-days, more than in times past, to maintain their greatness, and safety of their subjects, who if they have not wit or will to consider their own interest, so much your Majesty's wisdom must repair their defects, and force them by compulsion. But I hope there shall be no such cause in points so reasonable

I o increase your Majesty's revenue, I set down divers means for your gracious self to make choice of either, all or part at your pleasure, and to put in execution by such degrees and conditions as your great wisdom shall think fit in a business of this nature

Imprimis, The first course or means intended to increase your Majesty's revenues or profit withal, is of greatest consequence and I shall call it a *decima*, being so termed in Italy, where in some parts it is in use, importing the tenth part of all subjects estates, to be paid as a yearly rent to the prince, and as well moneyed men in towns, as landed men in the countries, their value and estates esteemed justly as it is to the true value, (though with reason), and this paid yearly in money . which course applied in England for your Majesty's service, may serve instead of subsidies, fifteens, and such like, which in this case are fit to be released for the subjects benefit and content. in recompence of the said *decima,* which will yield your Majesty more in certainty, than they do casually, by five hundred thousand pounds *per annum*, at the least.

Item, That when your Majesty hath gotten money into your hands by some courses to be set down, it would be a profitable course to

253

increase your *intrato*, to buy out all estates and leases upon your own lands, in such sort that they be made no losers, whereby, having your lands free, and renting them out to the true value, as it is most in use, and not employed as heretofore, at an old rent and small fines, you may rent it out for at least four or five times more money than the old rent comes to, so that if your Majesty's lands be already but threescore thousand pounds *per annum*, by this course it will be augmented at least two hundred thousand pounds *per annum*, and to buy out the tenants estates, will come to a small matter by the course, to make them no losers, considering the gains they have already made upon the lands and this is the rather to be done, and the present course changed, because it hath been a custom merely to cozen the King

Item, Whereas most princes do receive the benefit of salt in their own hands, as a matter of great profit, because they receive it at the lowest price possible, and vent it with double gains yearly, the same course used by your Majesty were worth an hundred and fifty thousand pounds at least It is likewise in other parts, that all weights and measures of the land, either in private houses, shops, or public markets, should be viewed to be just, and sealed once a-year, paying to the prince for it, which in England applied to your Majesty, with order to pay six pence for the sealing of each said weight or measure, would yield near threescore thousand pounds *per annum*

Item, That all counties pay a *gabella* for transportation of cloth, and so likewise in England, yet in Spain there is an impost upon the wools, which is so great a benefit and wealth to the sheep-masters, as they may well pay you 5 *l per cent* of the true value of their shearing, which I conceive may be worth 15,000 *l per annum.*

Item, Whereas the lawyers fees and gains in England be excessive, to your Majesty's subjects prejudice, it were to your Majesty to make use thereof, and to impose on all causes sentenced with the party, to pay 5 *l per cent* of the true value that the cause had gained him, and for a recompence thereof, to limit all lawyers fees and gettings, whereby the subject shall save more in fees and charges than he giveth in the *gabella*, which, I believe, may be worth one year with another fifty thousand pounds.

254

Item, Whereas the inns and victualling-houses in England are more chargeable to travellers than in other countries, it were good for your Majesty to limit them to certain ordinaries, and raise besides a large imposition, as it is used in Tuscany and other parts, that is, prohibiting all inns and victualling houses, but such as shall pay it, and to impose upon the chief inns and taverns to pay ten pounds a-year to your Majesty, and the worst five pounds *per annum*, and all the ale-houses twenty shillings *per annum*, more or less as they are in custom of all sorts. There are so many in England, that this impost will yield 100,000 *l per annum* to your Majesty

Item, In Tuscany and other parts there is a *gabella* of all cattle or flesh, or horses, sold in the market, paying three or four pound *per cent* for what they are sold for, which, by conjecture, may be worth in England 20,000 *l. per annum*, using the like custom upon fish and other victuals, bread excepted   And for this cause all flesh, and fish and victuals, to be praised and sold by weight, whereby the subject saveth more in not being cozened, than the imposition importeth them.

Item, In Tuscany is used a taxation of 7 *l per cent* upon all alienations of lands to the true value, as also seven pounds *per cent* upon all dowries or marriage-monies, the like, if it be justly used in England, were worth at least 100,000 *l per annum*, with many other taxations upon meal, and upon all merchandize in all towns, as well port-towns, which here I omit, as not fit for England   And, in satisfaction to the subjects for these taxes, your Majesty may be pleased to release them of wardships, and to enjoy their estates at 18 years old, and in the mean time their profit to be preserved for their own benefit   And also in forfeiture of estates by condemnation, your Majesty may release the subject, as not to take the forfeiture of their lands, but their goods, (high treason only excepted), and to allow the counsel of lawyers in cases of life and death, as also not to be condemned without two witnesses, with such like benefits, which import much more their good, than all the taxations named can prejudice them.

Item, That some of the former taxations be used in Scotland and Ireland, as may easily be brought about by the first example thereof

255

used in England, may very well be made to increase your revenue there, more than it is by 200,000 *l. per ann*

Item, All officers in the land, great and small, in your Majesty's grant, may be granted with condition to pay you a part yearly according to the true value. This in time may be worth, as I conceive, an hundred thousand pounds *per annum* Adding also notaries, attornies, and such like, to pay some proportion yearly towards it, for being allowed by your Majesty to practise, and prohibiting else any to practise in such places

Item, I know an assured course in your Majesty's navy, which may save at least forty thousand pounds *per annum*, which requiring a whole discourse by itself, I omit, only do promise you to do it whensover you command

Item, To reduce your Majesty's houshold to board-wages, as most other princes do, reserving some few tables. This will save your Majesty 60,000 *l per annum*, and ease greatly the subjects besides, both in carriages and provision, which is a good reason that your Majesty in honour might do it

Item, Whereas your Majesty's laws do command the strict keeping of fasting-days, you may also prohibit on those days to eat eggs, cheese, or white meats. but such only as are contented to pay 18 *d per annum*, for their liberty to eat them, and the better sort 10 *s* The employment of this may be for the defence of the land, in maintaining the navy, garrisons, and such like, much after the fashion of a *cruzado* in Spain, as your Majesty knoweth

Lastly, I have a course upon Catholics, and very safe for your Majesty, being with their good liking, as it may be wrought to yield you presently at least 200,000 *l per annum*, by raising a certain value upon their lands, and some other impositions, which requiring a long discourse by itself, I will omit it here, setting it down in my instructions It will save your Majesty at the least 10,000 *l per annum*, to make it pain of death, and confiscation of goods and lands, for any of the officers to cozen you, which now is much to be feared they do, or else they could not be so rich, and herein to allow a fourth part benefit to them that shall find out the cozenage

256

Here is not meant officers of state, as the Lord Treasurer, &c , being officers of the crown The sum of all this amounteth to two millions and two hundred thousand pounds *per annum.* Suppose it be but one million and a half, as surely your Majesty may make by the courses set down , yet it is more than I promised in my letter for your Majesty's service, besides some sums of money in present by the courses following

Imprimis, By the Prince's marriage.

Secondly, To make all the Earls in England *Grandees,* as in Spain, and *Princips,* with such like privileges, and to pay 20,000 *l* a piece for it.

Thirdly, Also, if you make them feodaries of the towns belonging to their Earldoms, if they will for it ——————— besides, as they do to the King of Spain in the kingdom of Naples , and so likewise Barons to be made Earls and Peers, to pay nineteen thousand pounds a piece , I think it might yield five hundred thousand pounds, and oblige them more sure to your Majesty

Fourthly, To make choice of two hundred of the richest men in England in estate that be not Noblemen, and make them titular, as it is used in Naples, and paying for it , that is, a Duke thirty thousand pounds, a Marquis fifteen thousand pounds, an Earl ten thousand pounds, a Baron or Viscount five thousand pounds

It is to be understood, that ancient Nobility of Barons and Earls are to proceed these as Peers, though these be made Marquisses or Dukes This may raise a million of pounds, and more to your Majesty To make Gentlemen of low quality, and franklins, or rich farmers, Esquires, to preceed them, would yield your Majesty also a great sum of money in present

I know another course to yield your Majesty three hundred thousand pounds in money, which as yet the time serveth not to deliver, until your Majesty be resolved to proceed in some of the former courses , which till then I omit

Other courses also that may make present money, I shall study for your Majesty's service , and as I shall find them out, acquaint you withal

Lastly, To conclude all these discourses, by the application of this course used for your profit, that is not only the means to make you the richest King that ever England had, but also your safety augmented thereby to be most secure , besides what is shewed in the first part of this discourse, I mean by the occasion of the taxation, and raising of monies, your Majesty shall have cause and means to employ, in all places of the land, so many officers and ministers to be obliged to you for their own profit and interest, as nothing can be attempted against your person and Royal state over the land, but some of these shall in all probability have means to find it out and hinder it Besides, this course will repress many disorders and abuses in the public government, which were hard to be discovered by men indifferent.

To prohibit gorgeous and costly apparel to be worn but by persons of good quality, shall save the Gentry of the kingdom much more money than they shall be taxed to pay your Majesty

Thus withal I humbly take my leave, and kiss your gracious hands, desiring pardon for my errors I may commit herein

STRAFFORD

APPENDIX II

King CHARLES's Case:

OR,

An APPEAL to all rational men,

CONCERNING HIS

TRIAL

IN THE

HIGH COURT of JUSTICE.

Being, for the most part, that which was intended to have been delivered at the bar, if the King had pleaded to the charge, and put himself upon a fair trial

WITH

An additional opinion, concerning the death of King *James,* the loss of *Rochel,* and the blood of *Ireland*

By *JOHN COOK, of Gray's-Inn, Barrister.*

Justice is an excellent virtue
Reason is the life of the law.
Womanish pity to mourn for a tyrant,
Is a deceitful cruelty to a city

King CHARLES's Case.

May it please your Lordship,

MY Lord President, and this high court, erected for the most comprehensive, impartial, and glorious piece of justice, that ever was acted and executed upon the theatre of England, for the trying and judging of Charles Stuart, whom God in his wrath gave to be a King to this nation, and will, I trust, in great love, for his notorious prevarications and blood-guiltiness, take him away from us He that hath been the original of all injustice, and the principal author of more mischiefs to the free-born people of this nation, than the best arithmetician can well enumerate, stands now to give an account of his stewardship, and to receive the good of justice, for all the evil of his injustice and cruelty Had he ten thousand lives, they could not all satisfy for the numerous, horrid, and barbarous massacres of myriads and legions of innocent persons, which, by his commands, commissions and procurements, (or at least all the world must needs say, which he might have prevented, and he that suffers any man to be killed, when he may save his life without danger of his own, is a murderer), have been cruelly slain, and inhumanely murdered, in this renowned Albion Anglia hath been made an Aceldama, and her younger sister Ireland a land of ire and misery; and yet this hard-hearted man, as he went out of the court down the stairs, Jan 22, said, (as some of the guard told me, and others), That he was not troubled for any of the blood that had been shed, but for the blood of one man, (peradventure he meant Strafford) He was no more affected with a list that was brought in to Oxford of five or six thousand slain at Edgehill, than to read one of Ben Johnson's tragedies You gentlemen royalists that fought for him, if ye had lost your lives for his sake, you see he would have no more pitied you by his own confession, than you do a poor worm And yet what heart but would cleave, if it were a rock; melt, if it were ice, break, if it were flint, or dissolve, if it were a diamond, to consider that so

263

much precious Protestant blood should be shed in these three kingdoms, so many gallant, valiant men, of all sorts and conditions, to
be sacrificed, and lose their lives, and many of them to die so desperately in regard of their eternal conditions, and all this merely and
only for the satisfying and fulfilling of one man's sinful lust and
wicked will? A good shepherd is he that lays down his life, or ven-
tures it, to save the sheep: but for one to be so proudly wedded to
his own conceits, as so maliciously to oppose his private opinion
against the public judgment and reason of state, and to make head
against the parliament, who acknowledged him to be head thereof, so
far as to give him the honour of the Royal assent, in settling the
militia and safety of the people, I say, for a Protestant prince so
beloved at home, and feared abroad, that in love, and by gentle
means, might have had anything from the parliament, for him to
occasion the shedding of so much blood, for a pretended prerogative,
as hereafter will appear nothing in effect but to fix and perpetuate an
absolute tyranny, I can say no less, but, O Lucifer! from whence
art thou fallen? and what heretics are they in politics, that would
have had such a man to live? much more that think his actions to
have merited love and praise from heaven and earth? But now to
dissect the charge.

1   THat the Kings of England are trusted with a limited power
to govern by law, the whole stream and current of legal
authorities run so limpid and clear, that I should but weary those
that know it already, and trouble those that need not know the particular cases for it is one of the fundamentals of law, That the King
is not above the law, but the law above the King. I could easily
deraign it from 1 Edward III. to the jurisdiction of courts, that the
King has no more power or authority than what by law is concredited
and committed to him But the most famous authority is Fortescue,
Chancellor to Henry VI (and therefore undoubtedly would not clip
his master's prerogative), who most judicially takes a difference between a government wholly regal and seignoral, as in Turky,
Russia, France, Spain, &c, and a government politic and mixed,
where the law keeps the beam even between sovereignty and subjection, as in England, Denmark, Sweden, and Poland The first,
where the edict of a prince makes the law, resembles an impetuous

264

inundation of the waters, whereby the corn and hay, and other fruits of the earth, are spoiled, as when it is midwinter at midsummer the latter is like a sweet, smooth stream, running by the pleasant fields and meadows   That, by the law of England, the King ought not to impose any thing upon the people, or take anything away from them to the value of a farthing, but by common consent in parliaments or national meetings, and that the people, of common right, and by several statutes, ought to have parliaments yearly, or oftener, if need be, for the redress of public grievances, and for the enacting of good and wholsome laws, and repealing of old statutes of Omri which are prejudicial to the nation   and that the King hath not by law so much power as a justice of peace to commit any man to prison for any offence whatsoever, because all such matters were committed to proper courts and officers of justice, and if the King by his verbal command send for any person to come before him, if the party refused to attend, and the messenger endeavouring to force him, they fell to blows, if the messenger killed the party sent for, this by the law is murder in him, but if he killed the messenger, this was justifiable in him, being in his own defence, so as to sue forth a pardon of course ; these and many other cases of like nature are so clear and well known, that I will not presume to multiply particulars

That the King took an oath at his coronation, to preserve the peace of the nation, to do justice to all, and to keep and observe the laws which the people have, himself confesses   And it was charged upon the late Archbishop, that he emasculated the oath, and left out very material words, *which the people shall chuse*[1] ; which certainly he durst not have done, without the King's special command   and it seems to me no light presumption, that from that very day he had a design to alter and subvert the fundamental laws, and to introduce an arbitrary and tyrannical government   But though there had been no oath, yet, by special office and duty of his place, every King of England is obliged to act for the people's good   for all power, as it is originally in the people, (he must needs be extreme ignorant, malicious, or a self-destroyer, that shall deny it), so it is given forth for their preservation, nothing for their destruction   for a King to rule by

[1] 1 Book of ord fol

lust, and not by law, is a creature that was never of God's making, not of God's approbation, but his permission And though such men are said to be gods on earth, it is in no other sense than the devil is called the god of this world. It seems, that one passage which the King would have offered to the court, (which was not permitted him to dispute the supreme authority in the nation, and standing mute, the charge being for high treason, it is a conviction in law), was, that 1 *Sam* viii is a copy of the king's commission, by virtue whereof, he, as King, might rule and govern as he list, that he might take the people's sons, and appoint them for himself, for his chariots, and to be his horsemen, and take their daughters to be his confectionaries, and take their fields and vineyards, and olive-yards, even the best of them, and their goodliest young men, and their asses, and give them to his officers, and to his servants which indeed is a copy and pattern of an absolute tyrant, and absolute slaves, where the people have no more than the tyrant will afford them. The Holy Spirit in that chapter does not insinuate what a good King ought to do, but what a wicked King would presume to do Besides, Saul and David had extraordinary callings, but all just power is now derived from, and conferred by the people. Yet, in the case of Saul, it is observable, that the people, out of pride to be like other nations, desired a King, and such a King as the Heathens had, which were all tyrants for they that know any thing in history, know, that the first four monarchs were all tyrants at first, till they gained the people's consent Nimrod the great hunter was Ninus that built Nineveh, the first tyrant and conqueror that had no title, and so were all kingdoms which are not elective, till the people's subsequent consent And though it be by descent, yet it is a continuation of a conquest. Till the people consent, and voluntarily submit to a government, they are but slaves, and in reason they may free themselves if they can In France the King begins his reign from the day of his coronation The Archbishop asks the people, If he shall be King The twelve peers, or some that personate them, say, *Yes* They gird the sword about him, then he swears to defend the laws. And is anything more natural than to keep an oath? And though virtuous Kings have prevailed with the people to make their crowns hereditary; yet the coronation shews the shell that the kernel hath been in Samuel was a good judge, and there was nothing could be

266

objected against him, therefore God was displeased at their inordinate desire of a King. And it seems to me, that the Lord declares his dislike of all such Kings as the Heathens were, that is, Kings with an unlimited power, that are not tied to laws for he gave them a King in his wrath therein dealing with them as the wise physician with the distempered and impatient patient, who desiring to drink wine, tells him the danger of inflammation, yet wine he will have, and the physician considering a little wine will do but little hurt, rather than his patient by fretting should take greater hurt, prescribes a little white wine, wherein the physician doth not approve his drinking of wine, but of two evils chuseth the least The Jews would have a King for majesty and splendor, like the Heathens. God permits this, he approves it not It seems to me, that the Lord renounces the very genus of such Kings as are there mentioned. And the old word *conning* (by contraction *King*) does not signify power or force to do what he will, but a knowing wise, discreet man, that opens the people's eyes, and does not lead them by the noses, but govern them with wisdom and discretion for their own good Therefore, gentlemen royalists, be not so mad as to misconstrue, either the oaths of allegiance or supremacy, or any league or covenant, that any man should swear to give any one leave to cut his throat The true meaning is, that the King of England was supreme in this land, in opposition to the Pope, or any other prince or potentate, as the words of the oath do import, *That no foreign state, prince, or potentate*, &c. In case of any foreign invasion, the King was by law to be generalissimo, to command the people for their own safety, and so it was expounded by the parliament in 13 Eliz which, for some reason of state, was not permitted to be printed with the statutes Besides, God told those Kings whom he had formerly anointed what their duty was, not to exalt themselves overmuch above their brethren, to delight themselves in the law of God Out of which I infer, that the Turks, Tartars, Muscovites, French, Spaniards, and all people that live at the beck and nod of tyrannical men, may and ought to free themselves from that tyranny, if, and when they can for such tyrants that so domineer with a rod of iron, do not govern by God's permissive hand of approbation or benediction, but by the permissive hand of his providence, suffering them to scourge the people, for ends best known to himself, until

he open a way for the people to work out their own infranchise-
ments

But before I speak of the war, it will be necessary, for the satisfaction of rational men, to open and prove the King's wicked design,
wherewith he stands charged   Now, that he had from the beginning
of his reign such a design and endeavour, so to tear up the founda-
tions of government that law should be no protection to any man's
person or estate, will clearly appear by what follows

1   By his not taking the oath so fully as his predecessors did , that
so, when the parliament should tender good laws to him for the
Royal assent, he might readily answer, that he was not by oath
obliged to confirm or corroborate the same

2. By his dishonourable and perfidious dealing with the people at
his coronation, when he set forth a proclamation, that, in regard of
the infection then spread through the kingdom, he promised to dispense with those knights that by an old statute were to attend at the
coronation, who were thereby required not to attend , but did, notwithstanding, within few months after take advantage of their absence,
and raised a vast sum of money out of their estates at the council-
table ; where they pleading the said proclamation for their justification, they were answered, That the law of the land was above any
proclamation like that tyrant, that when he could not by law execute
a virgin, commanded her to be deflowered, and then put to death.

3 By his altering the patents and commissions to the judges,
which having heretofore had their places granted to them so long as
they should behave themselves well therein, he made them but
during pleasure , that so, if the judges should not declare the law to
be as he would have it, he might with a wet finger remove them,
and put in such as should not only say, but swear, if need were, that
the law was as the King would have it.   For when a man shall give
five or ten thousand pounds for a judge's place during the King's
pleasure, and he shall the next day send to him to know his opinion,
of a difference in law between the King and a subject , and it shall
be intimated unto him, that if he do not deliver his opinion for the

268

King, he is likely to be removed out of his place the next day, which
if so, he knows not how to live, but must rot in prison for the money
which he borrowed to buy his place, as was well known to be some
of their cases, who underhand and closely bought great places, (to
elude the danger of the statute), whether this was not too heavy a
temptation for the shoulders of most men to bear, is no hard matter
to determine . so as, upon the matter, that very act of his made the
King at the least a potential tyrant. For when that shall be law
which a King shall declare himself, or which shall be declared by
those whom he chuses, this brings the people to the very next step
to slavery

But that which does irrefragably prove the design, was his restless
desire to destroy parliaments, or to make them useless   and for that,
who knows not but that there were three or four national meetings
in parliament in the first four years of his reign, which were called
for supply to bring money into his coffers in point of subsidies, rather
than for any benefit to the people ? as may appear by the few good
laws that were then made   But that which is most memorable, is
the untimely dissolving of the parliament in 4 Car when Sir John
Elliot, and others, (who managed a conference with the house of
Peers concerning the Duke of Buckingham, who, amongst other
things, was charged concerning the death of K James), were committed close prisoner to the Tower, where he lost his life by cruel
endurance   Which I may not pass over without a special animad-
version   for sure there is no Turk or Heathen but will say, that if
he were any way guilty of his father's death, let him die for it.

I would not willingly be so injurious to the honest reader, as to
make him buy that again which he had formerly met with in the
parliament's declaration or elsewhere, in such a case a marginal
reference may be sufficient   Nor would I herein be so presumptuous, as to prevent any thing that happily may be intended in any
declaration for more general satisfaction, but humbly offer a student's
mite, which satisfies myself, with submission to better judgments.

How the King first came to the crown, God and his own conscience best knew   It was well known and observed at court, that a

269

little before he was a professed enemy to the Duke of Buckingham;
but instantly upon the death of K James, took him into such special
protection, grace and favour, that upon the matter he divided the
kingdom with him   And when the Earl of Bristol had exhibited a
charge against the said Duke, the 13th article whereof concerned the
death of K. James, he instantly dissolved that parliament, that so
he might protect the Duke from the justice thereof, and would never
suffer any legal inquiry to be made for his father's death   The Rab-
bins observe, that that which stuck most with Abraham about God's
command to sacrifice Isaac, was this "Can 1 not be obedient,
"unless I be unnatural? What will the Heathens say, when they
"hear I have killed my only son?" What will an Indian say to this
case? A King hath all power in his hands to do justice, there is
one accused, upon strong presumptions at the least, for poisoning
that King's father, the King protects him from justice   whether do
you believe that himself had any hand in his father's death? Had
the Duke been accused for the death of a beggar, he ought not to
have protected him from a judicial trial. We know, that by law it
is no less than misprison of treason to conceal a treason, and to conceal a murder, strongly implies a guilt thereof, and makes him a kind
of accessary to the fact   He that hath no nature to do justice to his
own father, could it ever be expected that he should do justice to
others? Was he fit to continue a father to the people, who was without natural affection to his own father? Will he love a kingdom,
that shewed no love to himself, unless it was that he durst not suffer
inquisition to be made for it? But I leave it as a riddle, which at
the day of judgment will be expounded and unriddled, for some sins
will not be made manifest till that day with this only, that had he
made the law of God his delight, and studied therein night and day,
as God commanded his kings to do, or had he but studied Scripture
half so much as Ben Johnson or Shakespear, he might have learned,
that when Amaziah was settled in the kingdom, he suddenly did
justice upon those servants which had killed his father Joash[1] he
did not by any pretended prerogative excuse or protect them, but delivered them up into the hands of that justice which the horridness
of the fact did undoubtedly demerit

[1] 2 Kings xii 20 & xiv 1 5

That parliament[1] 4 Car. proving so abortive, the King sets forth a proclamation[2], that none should presume to move him to call parliaments, for he knew how to raise moneys enough without the help of parliaments   Therefore in twelve years he refuseth to call any.   In which interval and intermission, how he had oppressed the people by incroachments and usurpations upon their liberties and properties, and what vast sums of money he had forcibly exacted and exhausted by illegal patents and monoplies of all sorts, I refer the reader to that most judicious and full *declaration of the state of the kingdom*, published in the beginning of this parliament   That judgment of ship-money did upon the matter formalize the people absolute slaves, and him an absolute tyrant   for if the King may take from the people in case of necessity and himself shall be judge of that necessity, then cannot any man say that he is worth sixpence.   For if the King say that he hath need of that sixpence, then by law he must have it, I mean that great Nimrod, that would have made all England a forest, and the people which the Bishop calls his sheep, to be his venison to be hunted at his pleasure

Nor does the common objection, "That the judges and evil coun-"sellors, and not the King, ought to be responsible for such mal-"administrations, injustice, and oppression," bear the weight of a feather in the balance of right reason   For, 1 Who made such wicked and corrupt judges ? were they not his own creatures ? and ought not every man to be accountable for the works of his own hands ?   He that does not hinder the doing of evil, if it lies in his power to prevent it, is guilty of it as a commander thereof   He that suffered those black stars to inflict such barbarous cruelties, and unheard-of punishments, as branding, slitting of noses, &c, upon honest men, to the dishonour of the Protestant religion, and disgrace of the image of God shining in the face of man, he well deserved to have been so served.   But, 2 He had the benefit of those illegal fines and judgments.   I agree, that if a judge shall oppress I S for the benefit of I D the King ought not to answer for this, but the judge, unless he protect the judge against the complaint of I S , and in that case he makes himself guilty of it   But when an unjust judgment is given against I S for the King's benefit, and the fine to come immediately

[1] 27 Mar   [2] 5 Car

into his coffers, he that receives the money, must needs be presumed
to consent to the judgment   But, 3 Mark a Machiavel policy
" Call no parliaments to question the injustice and corruption of
" judges for the people's relief, and make your own judges, and let
" that be law that they declare , whether it be reasonable or unrea-
" sonable, it is no matter "

But then, how came it to pass that we had any more parliaments ?
Had we not a gracious King to call a parliament when there was so
much need of it, and to pass so many gracious acts to put down the
Star-chamber, &c. ?   Nothing less   It was not any voluntary free
act of grace, not the least ingredient or tincture of love or good affection to the people, that called the short parliament in 1640 , but to
serve his own turn against the Scots, whom he then had designed to
inslave.   And those seven acts of grace which the King passed, were
no more than his duty to do, nor half so much, but giving the
people a take of their own grists , and he dissents with them about
the militia, which commanded all the rest   He never intended
thereby any more good and security to the people, than he that steal-
ing the goose, leaves the feathers behind him   But to answer the
question, thus it was

The King being wholly given up to be led by the counsels of a
Jesuited party, who endeavoured to throw a bone of dissension
among us, that they might cast in their net into our troubled waters,
and catch more fish · for St Peter's see persuaded the King to set up
a new form of prayer in Scotland, and laid the bait so cunningly,
that, whether they saw it or not, they were undone   if they saw the
mystery of iniquity couched in it, they would resist, and so merit
punishment for rebelling , if they swallowed it, it would make way
for worse   Well, they saw the poison, and refused to taste it .   the
King makes war , and many that loved honour and wealth more than
God, assisted him   Down he went with an army, but his treasure
wasted in a short time   Fight they would not, for fear of an after
reckoning   Some commanders propound, that they should make
their demands , and the King grants all, comes back to London, and
burns the pacification, saying it was counterfeit   They re-assume
their forts , he raises a second war against them, and was necessi-

tated to call a parliament, offering to lay down ship-money for twelve
subsidies   They refuse   The King in high displeasure breaks off
the parliament, and in a declaration commands them not to think of
any more parliaments, for he would never call another.

There was a King of Egypt that cruelly oppressed the people.
They (poor slaves) complaining to one another, he feared a rising,
and commanded that none should complain upon pain of cruel
death.   Spies being abroad, they often met, but durst not speak, but
parted with tears in their eyes ; which declared, that they had more
to utter, but durst not.   This struck him to greater fears.   He commanded, that none should look upon one another's eyes at parting.
Therefore their griefs being too great to be smothered, they fetched
a deep sigh when they parted, which moved them so to compassion-
ate one another's wrongs, that they ran in and killed the tyrant.
The long hatching Irish treason was now ripe ; and therefore it was
necessary that England and Scotland should be in combustion, lest
we might help the Irish Protestants.   Well, the Scots get Newcastle.
He knew they would trust him no more, he had so often broke with
them, therefore no hopes to get them out by a treaty.   Many lords
and the city petition for a parliament   The King was at such a
necessity, that yield he must to that which he most abhorred.   God
had brought him to such a strait, he that a few months before
assumed the power of God, commanding men not to think of parliaments, to restrain the free thoughts of the heart of man, was constrained to call one   which they new he would break off when the
Scots were sent home, therefore got a confirmation of it, that he
should not dissolve it without the consent of both houses, of which
he had no hopes, or by force, which he suddenly attempted, and
the English army in the north was to have come up to confound the
parliament, and this rebellious and disloyal city, as the King called
it, and for their pains was promised thirty thousand pounds, and the
plunder, as by the examinations of Colonel Goring, Legge, &c. doth
more fully appear

And here, by the way, I cannot but commend the city-malignants.
He calls them rebels, they call him a gracious King : he by his proclamation at Oxford prohibits all commerce and intercourse of trade

273

between this populous city, (the life and interest whereof consists in
trade, without which many thousands cannot subsist), and other parts
of the kingdom, still they do good against evil, and petitioning him
so often to cut their throats, are troubled at nothing so much, as that
they are not reduced to that former and a worse bondage than when
there was a Lord Warden made in the city[1], and the King sent for
as much of their estates as he pleased   But surely the Oxfordshire
men are more to be commended   for when the King had commanded by his proclamation[2], that what corn, hay, and other provision, in the county of Oxford, could not be fetched into the said city
for his garrison, should be consumed and destroyed by fire, for fear
it should fall into the hands of the parliament's friends, a cruelty
not to be parallelled by an Infidel, Heathen, or Pagan King, nor to
be precedented amongst the most avowed and professed enemies,
much less from a King to his subjects, they resolved never to trust
him any more

But the great question will be, What hath been the true ground
and occasion of the war? which unless I clear, and put it out of
question, as the charge imports, I shall fall short of what I chiefly
aim at, *viz* "That the King set up his standard of war, for the
" advancement and upholding of his personal interest, power, and
" pretended prerogative, against the public interest of common right,
" peace and safety "   And thus I prove it

1. He fought for the militia by sea and land, to have it at his
absolute dispose, and to justify and maintain his illegal commissions
of array, and this he pretended was his birthright by the law of
England which if it were so, then might he by the same reason
command all the money in the kingdom, for he that carries the
sword, will command the purse

2 The next thing that he pretended to fight for, was his power to
call parliaments when he pleased, and dissolve them when he list
If they will serve his turn, then they may sit by a law to inslave the
people, so that the people had better chuse all the courtiers and
King's favourites at first, than to trouble themselves with ludibrious

[1] Darlingrub   [2] 15 April, 20 Car

274

elections to assemble the freeholders together, to their great labour, and expence both of time and coin, and those which are chosen knights and burgesses, to make great preparations, to take long journies to London themselves and their attendants, to see the King and Lords in their parliament-robes ride in state to the house, and, with Domitian, to catch flies and no sooner shall there be any breathings, or a spirit of justice stirring and discovered in the house of Commons, but the King sends the black rod, and dissolves the parliament; and sends them back again as wise as they were before, but not with so much money in their purses, to tell stories to the freeholders of the bravery of the King and Lords.

3 Well, but if this be too gross, and that the people begin to murmur and clamour for another parliament, then there goes out another summons, and they meet, and sit for some time, but to as much purpose as before. For when the Commons have presented any bill for redress of a public grievance, then the King hath several games to play to make all fruitless As, first, his own negative voice, that if Lords and Commons are both agreed, then he will advise, which, I know not by what strange doctrine, hath been of late construed to be a plain denial, though under favour at the first it was no more but to allow him two or three days time to consider of the equity of the law, in which time if he could not convince them of the injustice of it, then ought he by his oath and by law to consent to it

4 But if by this means the King had contracted hard thoughts from the people, and that not only the Commons, but many of the Lords, that have the same noble blood running in their veins as those English Barons, whose swords were the chief instruments that purchased magna charta, then, that the King might be sure to put some others between him and the people's hatred, the next prerogative that he pretended to have, was, to be the sole judge of chivalry, to have the sole power of conferring honours, to make as many Lords as he pleased, that so he may be sure to have two against one, if the house of Commons (by reason of the multitude of burgesses, which he likewise pretended a power to make as many borough towns and corporations as he pleased) were not packed also And this is that

275

glorious privilege of the English parliaments, so much admired for just nothing. For if his pretended prerogative might stand for law, as was challenged by his adherents, never was there a purer cheat put upon any people, nor a more ready way to inslave them, than by privilege of parliament, being just such a mockery of the people, as that mock parliament at Oxford was, where the King's consent must be the figure, and the representatives stand but for a cypher

5. But then out of parliament, the people are made to believe, that the King hath committed all justice to the judges, and distributed the execution thereof into several courts, and that the King cannot so much as imprison a man, nor impose any thing upon, nor take any thing away from the people, as by law he ought not to do. But now see what prerogative he challenges

1 If the King have a mind to have any public-spirited man removed out of the way, this man is killed, the murderer known, a letter comes to the judge, and it may be it shall be found but manslaughter If it be found murder, the man is condemned but the King grants him a pardon, which the judges will allow, if the word *murder* be in it but because it is too gross to pardon murder, therefore the King shall grant him a lease of his life for seven years, and then renew it, (like a Bishop's lease), as he did to Maj Prichard, who was lately justiced; who, being a servant to the Earl of Lindsey, murdered a Gentleman in Lincolnshire, and was condemned, and had a lease of his life from the King, as his own friends have credibly told me

2. For matter of liberty The King or any courtier sends a man to prison, if the judge set him at liberty, then put him out of his place, a temptation too heavy for those that love money and honour more than God to bear. therefore any judgment that is given between the King and a subject, it is not worth a rush, for what will not money do?

Next, He challenges a prerogative to inhance and debase money, which by law was allowed him, so far as to balance trade, and no further, that if gold went high beyond sea, it might not be cheap
276

here, to have it all bought up, and transported but, under colour of that, he challenges a prerogative, that the King may by proclamation make leather current, or make a sixpence go for twenty shillings, or a twenty shillings for sixpence which, not to mention any thing of the project of farthings or brass money, he that challenges such a prerogative, is a potential tyrant, for if he may make my twelve pence in my pocket worth but two pence, what property hath any man in any thing that he enjoys ?

Another prerogative pretended, was, That the King may avoid any grant, and so may cozen and cheat any man, by a law, the ground whereof is, That the King's grants shall be taken according to his intention, which, in a sober sense, I wish that all mens grants might be so construed according to their intentions, expressed by word or writing but by this means it being hard to know what the King intended, his grants have been, like the devil's oracles, taken in any contrary sense for his own advantage

Rep. 1. In the famous case of Altonwood's, there is vouched the Lord Lovel's case, that the King granted lands to the Lord Lovel and his heirs-male, not for service done, but for a valuable considera-tion of money paid   The patentee well hoped to have enjoyed the land, not only during his life, but that his heirs-male, at least of his body, should have likewise enjoyed it but the judges finding, it seems, that the King was willing to keep the money, and have his land again, (for what other reason, no mortal man can fathom), re-solved, that it was a void grant, and that nothing passed to the patentee   I might instance in many cases of like nature throughout all the reports, as one once made his boast, that he never made or passed any patent or charter from the crown, but he reserved one starting hole or other, and knew how to avoid it, and so merely to cozen and defraud the poor patentee   So that now put all these prerogatives together, 1. The militia by sea and land; 2 A liberty to call parliaments when he pleased, and to adjourn, prorogue or dissolve them at pleasure; 3 A negative voice, that the people can-not save themselves without him, and must cut their own throats, if commanded so to do, 4 The nomination and making of all the judges, that, upon peril of the loss of their places, must declare the
277

law to be as he pleases, 5 A power to confer honours upon whom, and how he pleases, a covetous base wretch for five or ten thousand pounds to be courted, who deserves to be carted, 6 To pardon murderers, whom the Lord says shall not be pardoned, 7 To set the value and price of monies as he pleases, that if he be to pay ten thousand pounds, he may make leather by his proclamation to be current that day, or a five shillings to pass for twenty shillings, and if to receive so much, a twenty shillings to pass for five shillings : and, lastly, A legal theft, to avoid his own grants I may boldly throw the gantlet, and challenge all the Machiavels in the world, to invent such an exquisite platform of tyrannical domination, and such a perfect tyranny without maim or blemish, as this is, and that by a law, which is worst of all, But the truth is, these are no legal prerogatives, but usurpations, incroachments and invasions upon the people's rights and liberties, and this easily effected without any great depth of policy for it is but being sure to call no parliaments, or make them useless, and make the judges places profitable, and place avarice upon the bench, and no doubt but the law shall sound as the King would have it But let me thus far satisfy the ingenuous reader, that all the judges in England cannot make one case to be law that is not reason, no more than they can prove a hair to be white that is black, which if they should so declare or adjudge, it is a mere nullity · for law must be reason adjudged, where reason is the *genus*, and the judgment in some court makes the *differentia*. And I never found, that the fair hand of the common law of England ever reached out any prerogative to the King above the meanest man, but in three cases. 1. In matters of honour and pre-eminence to his person, and in matters of interest, that he should have mines royal of gold and silver, in whose land soever they were discovered and fishes royal, as sturgeons and whales, in whose streams or water soever they were taken, which very rarely happened, or to have tithes out of a parish that no body else could challenge for says the law, "The most noble persons are to have the most noble things " 2 To have his patents freed from deceit, that he be not over-reached or cozened in his contracts, being employed about the great and arduous affairs of the kingdom. 3 His rights to be freed from incursion of time, not to be bound up by any statute of non-claim for indeed possession is a vain plea, when the matter of right is in question, for right can never die and some such honourable privileges of mending his plea, or suing in what court he will, and some such prerogatives of a middle indifferent nature, that could not be prejudicial to the people But that the law of England should give the King any such vast, immense, precipitating power, or any such god-like state, that he ought not to be accountable for wicked actions, or mal-administrations and mis-government, (as he hath challenged and averred in his answer to the petition of right), or any such principles of tyranny, which are as inconsistent with the people's liberties and safety, as the ark and Dagon, light and darkness, in an intensive degree, is a most vain and irrational thing to imagine And yet that was the ground of the war, as himself often declared; and that would not have half contented him, if he had come in by the sword But some rational men object, How can it be murder (say they) for the King to raise forces against the parliament? since there is no other way of determining differences between the King and his subjects but by the sword; for the law is no competent judge between two supreme powers. and then, if it be only a contending for each other's right, where is the malice, that makes the killing of a man murder? Take the answer thus First, How is it possible to imagine two supreme powers in one nation? no more than two suns in one firmament If the King be supreme, the parliament must be subordinate; if they supreme, then he subordinate But then it is alledged, That the King challenged a power only co-ordinate, that the parliament could do nothing without him, nor he without them. Under favour, two powers co-ordinate is as absurd as the other, for though in quiet times the Commons have waited upon the King, and allowed him a negative voice in matters of less concernment, where delay could not prove dangerous to the people, yet when the Commons shall vote that the kingdom is in danger, unless the militia be so and so settled, now if he will not agree to it, they are bound in duty to do it themselves. And it is impossible to imagine, that ever any man should have the consent of the people to be their King upon other conditions, without which no man ever had right to wear the diadem, for conquest makes a title amongst wolves and bears, but not amongst men

When the first agreement was concerning the power of parliaments,

if the King should have said, Gentlemen, are you content to allow
me any negative voice, that if you vote the kingdom to be in danger
unless such an act pass, if I refuse to assent, shall nothing be done
in that case? Surely no rational man but would have answered,
May it please your Majesty, we shall use all dutiful means to procure your Royal assent, but if you still refuse, we must not sit still
and see ourselves ruined, we must, and will save ourselves whether
you will or no And will any man say, that the King's power is
diminished, because he cannot hurt the people, or that a man is
less in health, that hath many physicians to attend him? God is
omnipotent, that cannot sin, and all power is for the people's good,
but a prince may not say that is for the people's good, which they
say and feel to be for their hurt And as for the malice, the law
implies that as when a thief sets upon a man to rob him, he hath
no spite to the man, but love to the money, but it is an implied
malice, that he will kill the people unless they will be slaves.

Quest But by what law is the King condemned?

Rep. By the fundamental law of this kingdom, by the general law
of all nations, and the unanimous consent of all rational men in the
world, written in every man's heart with the pen of a diamond in
capital letters, and a character so legible, that he that runs may read,
viz. That when any man is intrusted with the sword for the protection and preservation of the people, if this man shall employ it to
their destruction, which was put into his hand for their safety, by the
law of that land he becomes an enemy to that people, and deserves
the most exemplary and severe punishment that can be invented.
And this is the first necessary fundamental law of every kingdom,
which, by intrinsical rules of government, must preserve itself And
this law needed not be expressed, That if a King become a tyrant,
he shall die for it, it is so naturally implied We do not use to
make laws which are for the preservation of nature, that a man
should eat, and drink, and buy himself cloaths, and enjoy other
natural comforts, no kingdom ever made any laws for it And
as we are to defend ourselves naturally, without any written law,
from hunger and cold, so from outward violence. Therefore, if a
King would destroy a people, it is absurd and ridiculous to ask by

what law he is to die And this law of nature is the law of God written in the fleshly tables of mens hearts, that, like the elder sister, hath a prerogative right of power before any positive law whatsoever and this law of nature is an indubitable legislative authority of itself, that hath a suspensive power over all human laws If any man shall, by express covenant under hand and seal, give power to another man to kill him ; this is a void contract, being destructive to humanity. And by the law of England,[1] any act or agreement against the laws of God or nature, is a mere nullity · for as man hath no hand in the making of the laws of God or nature, no more hath he power to mar or alter them If the pilot of a ship be drunk, and running upon a rock , if the passengers cannot otherwise prevent it, they may throw him into the sea to cool him. And this question hath received resolution this parliament When the militia of an army is committed to a General, it is not with any express condition, That he shall not turn the mouths of his cannons against his own soldiers , for that is so naturally and necessarily implied, that it is needless to be expressed ; insomuch as, if he did attempt or command such a thing, against the nature of his trust and place, it did *ipso facto* estate the army in a right of disobedience , unless any man be so grossly ignorant to think, that obedience binds men to cut their own throats, or their companions. Nor is this any secret of the law which hath lain hid from the beginning, and now brought out, to bring him to justice ; but that which is co-natural with every man, and innate in his judgment and reason, and is as ancient as the first King, and an epidemical binding law in all nations in the world. For when many families agree, for the preservation of human society, to invest any King or Governor with power and authority , upon the acceptance thereof, there is a mutual trust and confidence between them, That the King shall improve his power for their good, and make it his work to procure their safeties , and they to provide for his honour , which is done to the commonwealth in him, as the sword and ensigns of honour carried before the Lord Mayor are for the honour of the city Now, as, when any one of this people shall compass the death of the Governor, ruling well, this is a treason punishable with death for the wrong done to the community, and anathema be to such a man so when he or they that are trusted to

[1] Com E. Leicester's case.

281

fight the people's battles, and to procure their welfare, shall prevari-
cate, and act to the inslaving or destroying of the people, who are
their liege-lords, and all governors are but the people's creatures, and
the work of their hands, to be accountable as their stewards, (and is
it not senseless for the vessel to ask the potter by what law he calls
it to account?); this is high treason with a witness, and far more
transcendent than in the former case, because the King was paid
for his service, and the dignity of the person does increase the
offence.   For a great man of noble education and knowledge to
betray so great a trust, and abuse so much love as the parliament
shewed to the King, by petitioning him as good subjects, praying for
him as good Christians, advising him as good counsellors, and treating with him as the great counsel of the kingdom, with such infinite
care and tenderness of his honour, (a course which God's people did
not take with Rehoboam; they never petitioned him, but advised
him, he refused their counsel, and hearkened to young counsellors,
and they cry, *To thy tents, O Israel*, and made quick and short work
of it), after all this, and much more longanimity and patience (which
God exercises towards man to bring him to repentance) from the
lord to the servant; for him not only to set up a standard of war in
defiance of his dread sovereign the people, (for so they truly were in
nature, though names have befoolled us), but to persist so many
years in such cruel persecutions, who with a word of his mouth
might have made a peace   if ever there were so superlative a treason,
let the Indians judge, and whosoever shall break and violate such a
trust and confidence, anathema Maranatha be unto them

Quest But why was there not a written law, to make it treason for
the King to destroy the people, as well as for a man to compass the
King's death?

Resp. Because our ancestors did never imagine, that any King of
England would have been so desperately mad, as to levy a war against
the parliament and people   As in the common instance of paricide,
the Romans made no law against him that should kill his father,
thinking no child would be so unnatural, to be the death of him who
was the author of his life   but when a child came to be accused for
a murder, there was a more cruel punishment inflicted, than for other
282

homicides for he was thrown into the sea in a great leather barrel, with a dog, a jackanapes, a cock, and a viper, significant companions for him, to be deprived of all the elements, as in my *Poor man's case, fol* 10 Nor was there any law made against parents that should kill their children ; yet if any man was so unnatural, he had an exemplary punishment

Obj. But is it not a maxim in law, *That the King can do no wrong ?*

Resp. For any man to say so, is blasphemy against the great God of truth and love for only God cannot err, because what he wills is right, because he wills it. And it is a sad thing to consider how learned men, for unworthy ends, should use such art to subdue the people, by transportation of their senses, as to make them believe that the law is, That the King can do no wrong.

1 For law, I do aver it with confidence, but in all humility, that there is no such case to be found in law, that if the King rob, or murder, or commit such horrid extravagancies, that it is no wrong. Indeed the case is put in Hen. VII by a chief judge, that "if the "King kill a man, it is no felony to make him suffer death ," that is to be meant in ordinary courts of justice but there is no doubt but the parliament might try the King, or appoint others to judge him for it. We find cases in law, that the King had been sued even in civil actions.

In 43 Edw. III 22. it is resolved, That all manner of actions did lie against the King, as against any Lord. And 24 Edw III. 23. Wilby, a learned judge, said, That there was a writ *Præcipe Henrico Regi Angliæ*

Indeed Edw I. did make an act of state, "That men should sue "to him by petition ," but this was not agreed unto in parliament, "Thelwall title roye digest of writs," 71 But after, when judges places grew great, the judges and bitesheeps began to sing lullaby, and speak Platentia to the King, that "My Lord the King is an angel of "light." Now, angels are not responsible to men, but God , therefore not kings. And the judges, they begin to make the King a

283

God, and say, That by law his style is *Sacred Majesty*, though he swears every hour, and *Gracious Majesty*, though gracious men be the chief objects of his hatred, and that the King hath an omnipotency and omnipresence

But I am sure there is no case in law, that if the King levy a war against the parliament and people, that it is not treason Possibly that case in Hen VII may prove, that if the King should in his passion kill a man, this shall not be felony to take away the King's life. for the inconveniency may be greater to the people, by putting a King to death for one offence and miscarriage, than the execution of justice upon him can advantage them But what is this to a levying of war against a parliament? Never any judge was so devoid of understanding, that he denied that to be treason. But suppose a judge that held his place at the King's pleasure did so, I am sure never any parliament said so. But what if there had, in dark times of Popery, been an act made, That the King might murder, ravish, burn, and perpetrate all mischiefs, and play reaks with impunity, will any man that hath but wit enough to measure an ell of cloth, or to tell twenty, say, That this is an obligation for men to stand still, and suffer a monster to cut their throats, and grant commission to rob at Suters-hill? As such, and no better are all legal thefts and oppressions The Doctor says, That a statute against giving an alms to a poor man is void He is no student, I mean, was never bound apprentice to Reason, that says, A King cannot commit treason against the people

Obj. But are there not negative words in the statute of 25 Edw III That nothing else shall be construed to be treason but what is there expressed?

Resp That statute was intended for the people's safety, that the King's judges should not make traitors by the dozens to gratify the King or courtiers; but it was never meant, to give liberty to the King to destroy the people And though it be said, That the King and parliament only may declare treason, yet, no doubt, if the King will neglect his duty, it may be so declared without him for when many are obliged to do any service, if some of them fail, the rest must do it

284

Obj But is there any precedent, that ever any man was put to death that did not offend against some written law? for where there is no law, there is no transgression.

Resp It is very true, where there is neither law of God, nor nature, nor positive law, there can be no transgression, and therefore that scripture is much abused to apply it only to laws positive.   For,

1   *Ad ea quæ frequentius,* &c. It is out of the sphere of all earthly lawgivers to comprehend and express all particular cases that may possibly happen, but such as are of most frequent concurrence, particulars being different, like the several faces of men different from one another, else laws would be too tedious and as particulars occur, rational men will reduce them to general reasons of state, so as everything may be adjudged for the good of the community

2. The law of England is, *Lex non scripta,* and we have a direction in the epistle to the 3d Rep That when our law books are silent, we must repair to the law of nature and reason Holinshed, and other historians, tell us, That in 20 Hen. VIII. the Lord Hungerford was executed for buggery, for which there was then no positive law to make it felony and before any statute against witchcraft, many witches have been hanged in England, because it is death by God's law.   If any Italian mountebank should come over hither, and give any man poison that should lie in his body above a year and a day and then kill him, (as it is reported they can give a man poison that shall consume the body in three years), will any make scruple or question to hang up such a rascal? At Naples, the great treasurer of corn being intrusted with many thousand quarters at three shillings the bushel, for the common good, finding an opportunity to sell it for five shillings the bushel to foreign merchants, inriched himself exceedingly thereby; and corn growing suddenly dear, the council called him to account for it, who profered to allow three shillings for it, as it was delivered into his custody, and hoped thereby to escape; but for so great a breach of trust, nothing would content the people but to have him hanged and though there was no positive law for it, to make it treason, yet it was resolved by the best politicians, that it was treason to break so great a trust by the fundamental

constitution of the kingdom , and that for so great an offence he ought
to die, that durst presume to inrich himself by that which might
indanger the lives of so many citizens for as society is natural, so
governors must of necessity, and in all reason, provide for the preservation and sustenance of the meanest member, he that is but as the
little toe of the body-politic.

But I know the ingenuous reader desires to hear something concerning Ireland, where there were no less than 152,000 men, women,
and children, most barbarously and fanatically murdered in the
first four months of the rebellion , as appeared by substantial proofs,
at the king's bench, at the trial of Macquire If the King had a
hand, or but a little finger in that massacre, every man will say, Let
him die the death But how shall we be assured of that? How
can we know the tree better than by its fruits? For my own
particular, I have spent many serious thoughts about it, and I desire
in doubtful cases to give charity the upper hand , but I cannot in
my conscience acquit him of it Many strong presumptions, and
several oaths of honest men, that have seen the King's commission
for it, cannot but amount to a clear proof If I meet a man running
down stairs with a bloody sword in his hand, and find a man stabbed
in the chamber , though I did not see this man run into the body by
that which I met, yet if I were of the jury, I durst not but find him
guilty of the murder. And I cannot but admire, that any man should
deny that for him, which he durst never deny for himself. How often
was that monstrous rebellion laid in his dish? and yet he durst
never absolutely deny it Never was bear so unwillingly brought to
the stake, as he was to declare against the rebels . and when he did
once call them rebels, he would suffer but forty copies to be printed,
and those to be sent to him sealed and he hath since above forty
times called them his subjects, and his good subjects, and sent to
Ormond to give special thanks to some of these rebels, as Muskerry
and Plunket, (which I am confident, by what I see of his height of
spirit and undaunted resolution at his trial and since, acting the last
part answerable to the former part of his life, he would rather have
lost his life, than to have sent thanks to two such incarnate devils, if
he had not been as guilty as themselves) , questionless, if the King
had not been guilty of that blood, he would have made a thousand
286

declarations against those blood-hounds and hell-hounds, that are not to be named but with fire and brimstone, and have sent to all princes in the world for assistance against such accursed devils in the shape of men. But he durst not offend those fiends and fire-brands, for if he had, I verily believe they would soon have produced his commission under his hand and seal of Scotland at Edinburgh 1641 A copy whereof is in the parliament's hands, attested by oath, dispersed by copies in Ireland, which caused the general rebellion

Obj He did not give commission to kill the English, but to take their forts, castles, towns, and arms, and come over and help him.

Resp. And is it like all this could be effected without the slaughter of the poor English? Did the King ever call them rebels, but in forty proclamations wrung out of him by force, by the parliament's importunity? murdering the Protestants was so acceptable to him, and with this limitation, that none should be published without his further directions, as appears under Nichols's hand, now in the parliament's custody. But the Scots were proclaimed rebels before they had killed a man, or had an army, and a prayer against them enjoined in all churches, but no such matter against the Irish

Well, when the rebels were worsted in Ireland, the King makes war here to protect them, which but for his fair words had been prevented, often calling God to witness, he would as soon raise war on his own children and men from Popish principles assist him. Well, we fought in jest, and were kept between winning and losing The King must not be too strong, lest he revenge himself, nor the parliament too strong, for the Commons would rule all, till Naseby fight, that then the King could keep no more days of thanksgiving so well as we Then he makes a cessation in Ireland, and many Irish came over to help him English came over with Papists, who had scarce wiped their swords since they had killed their wives and children, and had their estates.

But this I argue, The rebels knew that the King had proclaimed them traitors, and forty copies were printed and the first clause of an oath enjoined by the general council of rebels was, "To bear true

287

" faith and allegiance to King Charles, and by all means to main-
" tain his Royal prerogative against the Puritans in the parliament of
" England " Now, is any man so weak in his intellectuals, as to imagine, that if the rebels had, without the King's command or consent,
murdered so many Protestants, and he thereupon had really proclaimed them rebels, that they would after this have taken a new oath
to have maintained his prerogative? No, those bloody devils had
more wit than to fight in jest If the King had once in good earnest
proclaimed them rebels, they would have burnt their scabbards, and
would not have styled themselves *the King and Queen's army*, as they
did And truly, that which the King said for himself, That he would
have ventured himself to have gone in person into Ireland to suppress
that rebellion, is but a poor argument to enforce any man's belief,
that he was not guilty of the massacre for it makes me rather think,
that he had some hopes to have returned at the head of 20 or 30,000
rebels, to have destroyed this nation For when the Earl of Leicester
was sent by the parliament to subdue the rebels, did not the King
hinder him from going? and were not the cloaths and provisions which
were sent by the parliament, for the relief of the poor Protestants
there, seized upon by his command, and his men of war, and sold or
exchanged for arms and ammunition, to destroy this parliament?
And does not every man know, that the rebels in Ireland gave letters
of mart, for taking the parliament's ships, but freed the King's, as
their very good friends? And I have often heard it credibly reported,
that the King should say, That nothing more troubled him, but that
there was not as much Protestant blood running in England and
Scotland as in Ireland And when that horrid rebellion begun to
break forth, how did the Papists here triumph and boast, that they
hoped ere long to see London streets run down in blood? And yet
I do not think that the King was a Papist, or that he designed to introduce the Pope's supremacy in spiritual things into this kingdom
But thus it was, a Jesuitical party at court was too prevalent in his
councils, and some mungrel Protestants, that less hated the Papists
than the Puritans, by the Queen's mediation, joined all together to
destroy the Puritans, hoping that the Papists, and the Laodicean
Protestants, would agree well enough together And, lastly, if it be
said, That if the King and the rebels were never fallen out, what need
had Ormond to make a pacification or peace with them by the King's
288

commission, under the great seal of Ireland? Truly there hath been so much dawbing, and so little plain dealing, that I wonder how there comes to be so many beggars.

Concerning the betraying of Rochel, to the enslaving of the Protestant party in France, I confess, I heard so much of it, and was so shamefully reproached for it in Geneva, and by the Protestant Ministers in France, that I could believe no less than that the King was guilty of it   I have heard fearful exclamations from the French Protestants against the King, and the late Duke of Buckingham, for the betraying of Rochel   And some of the Ministers told me ten years since, That God would be revenged of the wicked King of England for betraying Rochel   And I have often heard Deodati say, concerning Henry IV. of France, That the Papists had his body, but the Protestants had his heart and soul, but for the King of England, The Protestants had his body, but the Papists had his heart   not that I think he did believe transubstantiation, (God forbid I should wrong the dead), but I verily believe, that he loved a Papist better than a Puritan

The Duke of Roan, who was an honest, gallant man, and the King's godfather, would often say, That all the blood which was shed in Dauphiny, would be cast upon the King of England's score   For thus it was, the King sent a letter to the Rochellers by Sir William Breecher, to assure them, that he would assist them to the uttermost against the French King, for the liberty of their religion, conditionally, that they would not make any peace without him, and Montague was sent into Savoy, and to the Duke of Roan, to assure them from the King, that 30,000 men should be sent out of England, to assist them against the French King, in three fleets, one to land in the isle of Ree, a second in the river of Bourdeaux, and a third in Normandy Whereupon the Duke of Roan, being General for the Protestants, not suspecting that the French durst assault him in Dauphiny, (because the King of England was ready to invade him, as he had promised), drew out his army upon disadvantage, whereupon the French King employed all his army in Dauphiny against the Protestants, who were forced to retreat, and the Duke of Roan to fly to Geneva, and the Protestants to accept of peace upon very hard conditions, to stand barely at the King's devotion for their liberties, without any cautionary towns of assurance, as formerly they had; being such a piece as the sheep make with the wolves when the dogs are dismissed   And the Protestants have ever since cried out to this very day, It is not the French King that did us wrong, for then we could have borne it, but it was the King of England, a professed Protestant, that betrayed us   And when I have many times entreated Deodati, and others, to have a good opinion of the King, he would answer me, That we are commanded to forgive our enemies, but not to forgive our friends.

There is a French book printed about two years since, called *Memoirs du Monsieur de Roan*, where the King's horrid perfidiousness and deep dissimulation is very clearly unfolded and discovered.   To instance but in some particulars, the King having solemnly engaged to the Rochellers, that he would hazard all the forces he had in his three kingdoms, rather than they should perish, did, in order thereunto, to gain credulity with them, send out eight ships to sea, commanded by Sir John Pennington, to assist the Rochellers, as was pretended , but nothing less intended : for Pennington assisted the French King against the Rochellers , which made Sir Ferdinando Gorge to go away with the Great Neptune, in detestation of so damnable a plot , and the English masters and owners of ships refusing to lend their ships to destroy the Rochellers, whom with their souls they desired to relieve, Pennington in a mad spite shot at them.

Subise, being agent here in England for the French Protestants, acquainted the King how basely Pennington had dealt , and that the English ships had mowed down the Rochel ships like grass, not only to the great danger and loss of the Rochellers, but to the eternal dishonour of this nation, scandal of our religion, and disadvantage of the general affairs of all the Protestants in Christendom   The King seems to be displeased, and says, What a knave is this Pennington ? But whether it was not feigned, let all the world judge   But the thing being so plain, said Subise to the King, Sir, why did the English ships assist the French King? and those that would not, were shot at by your Admiral   The French Protestants are no fools; how can I make them believe that you intend their welfare ?   The King

290

was much put to it for a ready answer, but at last thus it was packed up, that the French King had a design to be revenged of Genoa for some former affront, and that the King lent him eight English ships to be employed for Genoa, and that sailing towards Genoa, they met with some of the Rochellers accidentally and that the English did but look on, and could not help it, not having any commission to fight at that present wherein the Rochellers might, and would have declined a sea-fight, if they had not expected our assistance. But still the poor Protestants were willing, rather to blame Pennington than the King; who, in great seeming zeal, being surety for the last peace between the French King and his Protestant subjects, sends Devick to the Duke of Roan, to assure him, that if Rochel were not speedily set at liberty, (which the French King had besieged, contrary to his agreement), he would employ his whole strength, and in his own person see it performed · which being not done, then the King sends the Duke of Buckingham to the isle of Ree, and gives new hopes of better success to Subise, commanding the Admiral and officers in the fleet, in Subise's hearing, to do nothing without his advice. But when the Duke came to land at the isle of Ree, many gallant Englishmen lost their lives, and the Duke brought back 300 tuns of corn from the Rochellers, which he had borrowed of them, pretending a necessity for the Englishmen, which was but feigned, knowing it was a city impregnable, so long as they had provision within I confess the Rochellers were not wise to lend the Duke their corn, considering how they had been dealt with But what a base thing was it, so to betray them, and to swear unto them, that they should have corn enough sent from England before they wanted it? and for a long time, God did miraculously send them in a new kind of fish which they never had before But when the Duke came to court, he made the honest English believe, that Rochel would suddenly be relieved, and that there was not the least danger of the loss of it But Secretary Cook, an honest understanding gentleman, and the only friend at court to the Rochellers, labouring to improve his power to send some succour to Rochel, was suddenly sent away from court upon some sleeveless errand; or, as some say, to Portsmouth, under colour of providing corn for Rochel. But the Duke soon after went thither, and said, His life upon it, Rochel is safe enough And the next day, Subise being at Portsmouth, he pressed the Duke of

Buckingham most importunately to send relief to Rochel then or never; the Duke told him, that he had just then heard good news of the victualling of Rochel, which he was going to tell the King which Subise making doubt of, the Duke affirmed it by an oath, and having the words in his mouth, he was stabbed by Felton, and instantly died The poor Rochellers seeing themselves so betrayed, exclaimed of the English, and were constrained through famine to surrender the city Yet new assurances came from the King to the Duke of Roan, that he should never be abandoned, and that he should not be dismaid nor astonished for the loss of Rochel

But Subise spoke his mind freely at court, That the English had betrayed Rochel, and that the loss of that city was the apparent perdition and loss of thirty two places of strength from the French Protestants in Languedoc, Piedmont, and Dauphiny therefore it was thought fit that he should have a fig given him to stop his mouth Well, not long after, two capuchins were sent into England to kill honest Subise, and the one of them discovered the other Subise rewarded the discoverer, and demanded justice here against the other, who was a prisoner, but, by what means you may easily imagine, that assassinate rascal, instead of being whipped, or receiving some more severe punishment, was released, and sent back into France with money in his purse And one of the messengers that was sent from Rochel to complain of those abominable treacheries, was taken here, and, as the Duke of Roan writes, was hanged for some pretended felony or treason And much more to this purpose may be found in the Duke of Roan's memorials. But yet I know many wise, sober men do acquit the King from the guilt of the loss of Rochel, and lay it upon the Duke, as if it were but a loss of his reputation They say, that the Duke of Buckingham agitated his affairs, neither for religion, nor the honour of his master, but only, to satisfy his passion in certain foolish vows which he made in France, entered upon a war, and that the business miscarried through ignorance, and for want of understanding to manage so difficult a negotiation, he being unfit to be an Admiral or a General

I confess that for many years I was of that opinion, and thought that the King was seduced by evil counsel, and some thought, that
292

Buckingham, and others, ruled him as a child, and durst do what they list But certainly he was too politic and subtil a man to be swayed by anything but his own judgment Since Naseby letters, I ever thought him principal in all transactions of state, and the wisest about him but accessories He never acted by any implicit faith in state-matters , the proudest of them all durst never cross him in any design when he had once resolved upon it Is any man so soft-brained to think, that the Duke or Pennington durst betray Rochel without his command? would not he have hanged them up at their return, if they had wilfully transgressed his commands? A thousand such excuses made for him, are but like Irish quagmires, that have no solid ground or foundation in reason He was well known to be a great student in his younger days, that his father would say, He must make him a Bishop. He had more learning and dexterity in state-affairs, undoubtedly, than all the kings in Christendom If he had had grace answerable to his strong parts, he had been another Solomon , but his wit and knowledge proved like a sword in a mad-man's hand he was a stranger to the work of grace and the Spirit of God, as the poor creature confessed to Mr Knowles after he was condemned , and all those meanders in state, his serpentine turnings and windings, have but brought him to shame and confusion. But I am fully satisfied, none of his council durst ever advise him to any thing but what they knew before he resolved to have done and that they durst as well take a bear by the tooth, as do, or consent to the doing of any thing, but what they knew would please him They did but hew and square the timber , he was the master-builder that gave the form to every architecture. And being so able and judicious to discern of every man's merits, never think that the Duke or Pennington, or any judge or officer, did ever any thing for his advantage, without his command, against law or honour

Upon all which premisses, may it please your Lordship, I do humbly demand and pray the justice of this high court and yet not I, but the innocent blood that hath been shed in the three kingdoms, demands justice against him. This blood is vocal, and cries loud , and yet speaks no better, but much louder than the blood of Abel For what proportion hath the blood of that righteous man, to the blood of so many thousands? If King Ahab and Queen Jezebel,

for the blood of one righteous Naboth, (who would not sell his inheritance for the full value,) were justly put to death, what punishment does he deserve that is guilty of the blood of thousands,
and fought for a pretended prerogative, that he might have any
man's estate that he liked without paying for it? This blood hath
long cried, " How long, parliament, how long, army, will ye forbear
" to avenge our blood? Will ye not do justice upon the capital
" author of all injustice? When will ye take the proud lion by the
" beard, that defies you with imperious exultations? What is the
" house of Commons? what is the army? (as Pharaoh said, *Who is*
" *the Lord? and who is Moses?*), I am not accountable to any
" power on earth" Those that were murdered at Brainford, knocked
on the head in the water, and those honest souls that were killed in
cold blood at Bolton and Liverpool in Lancashire, at Bartomley in
Cheshire, and many other places, their blood cries night and day for
justice against him, their wives and children cry, " Justice upon the
" murderer, or else give us our fathers and husbands again," nay,
should the people be silent, the very stones and timber of the houses
would cry for justice against him But, my Lord, before I pray
judgment, I humbly crave leave to speak to two particulars 1 Concerning the prisoner. When I consider what he was, and how many
prayers have been made for him, though I know that all the world
cannot restore him, nor save his life, because God will not forgive
his temporal punishment, yet if God in him will be pleased to add
one example more to the church of his unchangeable love to his
elect in Christ, not knowing but that he may belong to the election
of grace, I am troubled in my spirit in regard of his eternal condition, for fear that he should depart this life, without love and reconciliation to all those saints whom he hath scorned under the notion
of Presbyterians, Anabaptists, Independents, and Sectaries It cannot be denied, but that he hath spent all his days in unmeasurable
pride, that, during his whole reign, he hath deported himself as a
God, been depended upon, and adored as God, that hath challenged and assumed an omnipotent power, an earthly omnipotence,
that with the breath of his mouth hath dissolved parliaments his
Non placet hath made all the counsels of that supreme court to
become abortives *Non curo* hath been his motto, who, instead of
being honoured as good kings ought to be, and no more, hath been

294

idolized and adored, as our good God only ought to be a man that hath shot all his arrows against the upright in the land, hated Christ in his members, swallowed down unrighteousness as the ox drinks water, esteemed the needy as his footstool, crushed honest public-spirited men, and grieved when he could not afflict the honest more than he did, counted it the best art and policy to suppress the righteous, and to give way to his courtiers so to gripe, grind, oppress and over-reach the free people of the land, that he might do what he list, (the remembrance whereof would pierce his soul, if he knew the preciousness of it). But all sins to an infinite mercy are equally pardonable, therefore my prayer for this poor wretch shall be, That God would so give him repentance to life, that he may believe in that Christ whom he hath imprisoned, persecuted and murdered in the saints; that he which hath lived a tyrant, and hated nothing so much as holiness, may die a convert, and in love to the saints in England; that so the tears of the oppressed and the afflicted may not be as so many fiery stinging serpents, causing an eternal despair-ing, continual horror to this miserable man, when all tyrants shall be astonished, and innocent blood will affright more than twelve legions of devils All the hurt that I wish to him, is, that he may look the saints in the face with comfort, for the saints must judge the world And however it may be he or his adherents may think it a brave Roman spirit, not to repent of any thing, nor express any sorrow for any sin, though never so horrid, taking more care and fear not to change their countenance upon the scaffold, than what shall become of them after death yet I beseech your Lordship, that I may tell him and all the malignants now living but this "Charles Stuart, " unless you depart this life in love and reconciliation to all those " saints and godly men whom you have either ignorantly or malici- " ously opposed, mocked and persecuted, and still scorn and jeer at " as heretics and sectaries, there is no more hopes for you ever to " see God in comfort, than for me to touch the heavens with my " finger, or with a word to annihilate this great building, or for the " devil to be saved, which he might be, if he could love a saint as " such." No, Sir, it will be too late for you to say to those saints whom you have defied, "Give me some of your holiness, that I may " behold God's angry countenance You can expect no answer, but, "Go, buy, Sir, of those soul-hucksters, your Bishops, which fed

295

" you with chaff and poison, and now you must feed upon fire and
" brimstone to all eternity "

2 Concerning myself, I bear no more malice to the man's person,
than I do to my dear father, but I hate that cursed principle of
tyranny that has so long lodged and harboured within him, which
has turned our waters of law into blood, and therefore upon that
malignant principle I hope this high court (which is an habitation
of justice, and a royal palace of principles of freedom) will do speedy
justice, that this lion, which has devoured so many sheep, may not
only be removed out of the way, but that this iron sceptre, which hath
been lifted up to break this poor nation in pieces like a potter's vessel,
may be wrested out of the hands of tyrants, that my honourable
clients (for whom I am an unworthy advocate) the people of England,
may not only taste, but drink abundantly of those sweet waters of
that well of liberty which this renowned army hath digged with their
swords, which was stopped by the Philistines, the fierce Jew, and un-
circumcised Canaanite The hopes whereof made me readily to
hearken to the call to this service, as if it had been immediately from
heaven, being fully satisfied, that the prisoner was long since condemned to die by God's law (which being more noble and ancient
than any law of man, if there had been a statute that he should not
die, yet he ought to be put to death notwithstanding), and that this
high court was but to pronounce the sentence and judgment written
against him And though I might have been sufficiently discouraged,
in respect that my reason is far less than others of my profession,
yet considering that there are but two things desirable to make a
dumb man eloquent, namely, A good cause, and good judges, the
first whereof procures the justice of heaven, and the second justice
upon earth, and thinking that happily God might make use of one
mean man at the bar, amongst other learned counsel, that more of
his mind might appear in it, (for many times the less there is of man,
the more God's glory doth appear, and hitherto very much of the
mind of God hath appeared in this action), I went as cheerfully about
it as to a wedding and that the glory of this administration may be
wholly given to God, I desire to observe, to the praise of his great
name, the work of God upon my own spirit, in his gracious assistance
and presence with me, as a return of prayer and fruit of faith, believ-

ing that God never calls to the acting of anything
so pleasing to him as this most excellent court
of justice is, but he is present with the honourable
judges, and those that wait upon them. I have
been sometimes of counsel against felons and
prisoners; but I never moved the court to proceed
to judgment against any felon, or to keep any
man in prison, but I trembled at it in my thoughts;
as thinking it would be easier to give an account
of mercy and indulgence, than of anything that
might look like rigour: but now my spirits are
quite of another temper; and I hope it is meat
and drink to good men to have justice done,
and recreation to think what benefit this nation
will receive by it.

And now, my Lord, I must, as the truth is, conclude
him guilty of more transcendent treasons, and
enormous crimes, than all the kings in this
part of the world have ever been. And as he
that would picture Venus, must take the eyes
of one, the cheeks of another beautiful
woman, and so other parts to make a compleat
beauty: so to delineate an absolute tyrant, the
cruelty of Richard III. and all the subtilty, treachery,
dissimulation, abominable projects, and dishonourable
shifts, that ever were separately in any that swayed
the English sceptre, conspired together to make
their habitation in this whited wall. Therefore
I humbly pray, that as he has made himself a
precedent in committing such horrid acts,
which former kings and ages knew not, and have
been afraid to think of, that your Lordship,
and this high court, out of your sublime wisdoms,

297

and for justice sake, would make him an
example for other kingdoms for the time to
come, that the kings of the earth may hear,
and fear, and do no more so wickedly;
that he which would not be a pattern of
virtue, and an example of justice in his
life, may be a precedent of justice to others
by his death

FINIS

Lightning Source UK Ltd.
Milton Keynes UK
UKHW020249201219
355694UK00006B/132/P

9 781376 842555